LOVE & LEMONS

— SIMPLE —

Feel Good

FOOD

LOVE &

SIM

Feel

FO

AVERY
an imprint of
Penguin Random
House
New York

LEMONS

PLE

Good

OD

125
Plant-Focused
Meals to Enjoy
Now or Make
Ahead

JEANINE
DONOFRIO

WITH PHOEBE MOORE

PHOTOGRAPHY
BY EVA KOLENKO

AVERY

an imprint of Penguin Random House LLC
penguinrandomhouse.com

Copyright © 2023 by Jeanine Donofrio

Photographs © 2023 by Eva Kolenko
Photographs on pages 8 and 262 © 2023 by Jack Mathews
Endpaper art © Shutterstock/logaryphmic

Most Avery books are available at special quantity discounts for bulk purchase for sales promotions, premiums, fundraising, and educational needs. Special books or book excerpts also can be created to fit specific needs. For details, write SpecialMarkets@penguinrandomhouse.com.

Library of Congress Cataloging-in-Publication Data

Names: Donofrio, Jeanine, author.
Title: Love and lemons: simple feel good food: 125 plant-focused meals to enjoy now or make ahead / Jeanine Donofrio.
Description: New York: Avery, an imprint of Penguin Random House, [2023] | Includes index.
Identifiers: LCCN 2022024974 (print) | LCCN 2022024975 (ebook) | ISBN 9780593419106 (hardcover) | ISBN 9780593419113 (epub)
Subjects: LCSH: Vegetarian cooking. | Quick and easy cooking. | Make-ahead cooking. | LCGFT: Cookbooks.
Classification: LCC TX837.D6323 2023 (print) | LCC TX837 (ebook) | DDC 641.5/636—dc23/eng/20220815
LC record available at https://lccn.loc.gov/2022024974
LC ebook record available at https://lccn.loc.gov/2022024975

Printed in China
10 9 8 7 6 5 4 3 2 1

Book and cover design: Make & Matter
Food stylist: Marian Cooper Cairns
Food styling assistant: Natalie Drobny
Prop stylists: Claire Mack and Suzie Holmstrom
Photo assistant: Brad Knilans

TO THE
LOVE & LEMONS
READERS

TABLE OF

CONTENTS

INTRODUCTION

My mom keeps a whole lasagna in her freezer at all times. My sister and brother-in-law plan and shop for their meals at the beginning of every week. I prefer to cook on the fly with what I bring home from the farmers market or with what I have on hand.

For a long time, I was convinced that my way was, of course, the best way. My cook-from-the-hip approach was fun and freeing, after all! I even wrote a book (*The Love & Lemons Cookbook*) about the impromptu meals that I made with my farmers market finds.

But over the last few years, I've finally realized that there isn't one best way to get dinner on the table. For one, I have an overall busier life (we have a baby now!). I have to admit, my mom is right—sometimes, a frozen lasagna can be a lifesaver on a hectic weeknight.

I've also learned from you—the Love & Lemons readers.

I've had countless conversations with you about your favorite recipes on loveandlemons.com, adapting recipes to make them work for you, and what you'd like to see more of. You've taught me that we all share a goal: to eat fresh, healthy, and delicious food. But, as with my family and me, we have different ways of getting there.

Some of you love easy meals that you can make right now. When I posted a tomato soup recipe that you could make with ingredients you had in your pantry right at that moment, you made it, right then.

Others of you like to plan ahead. When I shared a sweet potato grain bowl that you could prep in advance for lunch, you (and I!) enjoyed wholesome meals all week. When I wrote about how to put together one grocery list for three easy (but not identical) dinners, an overwhelming number of you said, "I'd love to see a book with this approach!"

So here we are. This book serves up feel-good recipes for these two types of cooks: those who love easy, at-the-ready dishes that can be made at the drop of a hat, and those who like to plan in advance. You might be one, the other, or a little bit of both. Whatever the case, I hope these recipes make your mealtimes simpler, fresher, and more delicious. Happy cooking!

WHAT TYPE *of* COOK ARE YOU?

This book is organized into sections by meal type: breakfast, salads, soups, dinner, and dessert. Each of these sections is divided into two types of recipes, which cater to two different types of cooks:

PART

1

AT THE READY

When dinnertime rolls around, you like to open the fridge and make something delicious with what you have on hand. Your favorite recipes are ones that take the flavor to the max while keeping the ingredients, the prep, and ideally the dishes(!) to a minimum.

PART

2

IN ADVANCE

For you, meal prep is the name of the game. You like to have a week's worth of vibrant salads queued up in the fridge for lunch, a tasty sauce ready for weeknight grain bowls, and a whole lasagna in the freezer for the next time you have company.

Maybe you think one of these cooking styles describes you perfectly. Or maybe you don't. That's okay too! These days, I think of myself as part one, part the other. On a busy weeknight, I might use what I have on hand to whip up Chickpea Cacio e Pepe (page 119), or I might pull some Spicy Red Lentil Sweet Potato Stew (page 85) out of the freezer and call it dinner. Both strategies are great ways to get a flavorful meal on the table. Stick to one if it works for you, or have fun alternating between the two! Either way, the recipes in this book will help you simplify the process of day-to-day cooking. You'll learn how to minimize time at the grocery store, utilize pantry ingredients, and, overall, become more efficient in the kitchen.

AT THE READY

An At the Ready
recipe . . .

- can be made in roughly
45 minutes or less.

- has a short ingredient
list made up of
everyday staples.

- is efficiently organized.
For example, you
might start roasting
the main component of
the recipe and make a
sauce while it cooks.

TIPS

Stock that pantry!
The better you stock your pantry, the more you can make with what you have on hand. With basic oils, vinegars, and other staples in your kitchen, you can improvise a grain bowl (see page 66) or veggie tacos (see page 130) using whatever produce you have on a given day. You can also save time at the grocery store. For example, if you keep orzo and vegetable broth around, you can just grab a bunch of asparagus and have Creamy Orzo with Asparagus & Peas (page 115) on the dinner table in no time. See page 21 for a list of ingredients that I like to keep on hand.

Embrace a few quick-cooking ingredients.
I love brown rice, wheat berries, and other whole grains, but many of them take more than 30 minutes to cook. So, when I want to make something filling, fast, I often turn to starches like couscous, pasta, and quick-cooking farro instead. You'll find them throughout the At the Ready recipes. I recommend keeping them in your pantry for simple weeknight cooking!

If you do one thing in advance . . .
Cook those whole grains ahead of time! Then, freeze them so that you'll have them on hand to quickly bulk up veggie meals.

IN ADVANCE

In Advance recipes
fall into one of these
three categories:

1. Recipes with components
that can be made ahead
and assembled when
you're ready to eat.

2. Recipes that can be
made entirely ahead
and also freeze well.

3. Recipes that share one
grocery list for three
dinners. In this section, the
components from the first
recipe flow into the second
and the third. There's some
meal prep on Day 1 so that
the cooking process is
streamlined on Days 2 and 3.

TIPS

Make room in your freezer.

If you're an In Advance cook, then your freezer is one of the most valuable tools in your kitchen. Prep a whole meal ahead of time, freeze it, and when you're ready to eat, all you have to do is pop it in the microwave or oven to reheat! The In Advance recipes include freezer-friendly dishes for every meal of the day—Lemon Cornmeal Scones (page 43), Mushroom Farro Kale Soup (page 87), a "Cheesy" Broccoli Bake (page 157), and more.

Get scrappy.

Often, kitchen "scraps" can be repurposed to make yummy meals down the road. When you come across a recipe that uses leeks or carrots but not their tops, freeze the scrap parts to make flavorful vegetable broths later on (see page 98). Have a few slices of stale bread? Turn them into bread crumbs to use in the Cozy Autumn Pasta Bake (page 125) or the Farro & Greens Gratin (page 198).

Get your storage containers ready.

No matter what kind of In Advance recipe you're making, a good supply of storage containers will serve you well. I like to use glass containers in the fridge and freezer. To prevent breakage, allow food to cool completely before freezing it, and don't overfill your containers. Leave at least an inch at the top of each container so that the food has room to expand in the freezer.

If you do one thing at the last minute . . .

Shop for produce in its peak season. Even though the In Advance recipes highlight meal prep hacks to get ahead, they're still packed with fresh produce. Get great tomatoes for the lentil bowls on page 218, and take a few minutes to pick up fresh herbs for the Farro Stuffed Zucchini on page 166 (or better yet, grow a few herbs yourself).

SO, WHAT IS
FEEL-GOOD FOOD?

While the recipes in this book are divided into the At the Ready and In Advance categories, they all yield what I like to call feel-good food. I realize that a phrase like "feel-good" can mean different things to different people, especially when it comes to food.

Here's what feel-good food means to me:

IT'S BUILT AROUND VEGETABLES.

Before I decide what to cook, I check my fridge to see what vegetables I have on hand. Then, I build from there. A broccoli grain bowl with a tasty sauce? Sweet potato veggie burgers with curry spices and paneer? This veggie-first approach sparks my creativity and guarantees that I'm eating plenty of vegetables, both of which make me feel good!

IT'S SEASONAL.

As much as possible (and weather depending!), I visit the farmers market for local, seasonal produce. That sesame tomato salad on page 49 will taste ten times better in August with local tomatoes than it will in January with out-of-season ones.

IT'S FUN TO MAKE.

You've probably guessed: I love to cook. After a day spent in front of the computer or too much time on my phone, I love the tactile experience of making something with my hands. To me, chopping is meditative, and simmering soup is soothing. When it comes to feel-good food, the cooking *process* is just as nourishing as the final dish.

IT SATISFIES A CRAVING.

Gone are the days of "good foods" and "bad foods." In the summer, I love big, refreshing salads. On a freezing-cold winter night, I want to savor something comforting, like a creamy baked pasta or the Butternut & Thyme Galette on page 145. You'll find both types of recipes in this book.

A WELL-STOCKED PANTRY MAKES COOKING MORE FUN!

The more pantry basics you keep on hand . . .

The less time you'll spend at the grocery store.
Grab some fresh produce (and any basics you need to restock),
and you'll have what you need to make delicious meals at home!

....

The more variety you'll find on your plate.
Different pantry staples allow you to explore different flavors and cooking
techniques, meaning that you won't get stuck eating the same thing on
repeat (unless you want to). Even something as basic as stocking up
on different types of oil can open up new possibilities in the kitchen.
Olive oil is fruity and flavorful, great for using in dressings or Italian or
Mediterranean recipes. Neutral avocado oil is better for high-heat cooking.
Coconut oil adds rich, slightly sweet notes to curries and desserts.

....

The more you'll be able to make what you really *want* to eat.
Do you ever have nights when you're craving something—say, pasta or
tacos—but you don't feel like going to the grocery store? Well, keep a box
of pasta in your pantry and tortillas in your freezer, and that last-minute
shopping trip won't be necessary. Pasta or tacos, coming right up!
A well-stocked pantry makes it easy to cook what sounds good to you.

HERE'S WHAT I KEEP IN MY PANTRY:

OILS & VINEGARS

extra-virgin olive oil
avocado oil
coconut oil
toasted sesame oil
apple cider vinegar
balsamic vinegar
distilled white vinegar
red wine vinegar
rice vinegar

SPICES

fine grain sea salt
flaky sea salt
black peppercorns
cardamom
chili powder
cinnamon
coriander
cumin, ground and seeds
curry powder
garlic powder
ground ginger
nutmeg
onion powder
oregano
red pepper flakes
smoked paprika
turmeric

BAKING

all-purpose flour
almond flour
whole wheat flour
whole rolled oats
baking powder
baking soda
cane sugar
brown sugar
honey
maple syrup
chocolate chips
ground flaxseed
vanilla extract

CANNED AND JARRED GOODS

beans
chickpeas
canned tomatoes
capers
full-fat coconut milk
jarred roasted red peppers
kalamata olives
marinara sauce
tahini

DRY GOODS

beans (see page 72)
grains (see page 70)
green or French green lentils
red lentils
dried noodles and pasta
nutritional yeast
panko bread crumbs
dried fruit
nuts and seeds
vegetable broth

FRIDGE

almond milk
Dijon mustard
eggs
feta cheese
Greek yogurt
lemons
limes
mayonnaise
pecorino cheese
sriracha
tamari
white miso paste

FREEZER

bread and bread crumbs
fresh ginger
tortillas

HOW TO MEASURE FLOUR

I love the anticipation involved in baking. As you whisk and measure wet and dry ingredients, catching a whiff of vanilla or the bright scent of lemon zest, you imagine how delicious the treats you're making are going to be.

So there's nothing more disappointing than when that loaf of banana bread, say, or those fresh-baked scones end up being dry.

But good news! There's an easy way to avoid this common baking problem. It all comes down to how you measure flour.

In the baking recipes in this book, you need to Spoon and Level your flour.

Here's what I mean:

- **DON'T scoop flour straight from the canister or bag!**
- **Instead, fluff it with a spoon and then gently spoon it into your measuring cup, being careful not to pack it down. It should form a small mound above the rim of your measuring cup.**
- **Clear off any excess flour by gently leveling the top with a knife.**

Why all the fuss? Well, it's easy for flour to become compacted. If you scoop it straight from the canister or bag without spooning and leveling it, you'll likely pack too much into your measuring cup. Using too much flour is the number one reason baked goods come out dry!

For baking success, use the spoon-and-level method every time.

BREAKFAST

Savory Tahini Yogurt Bowls

Whether you're a sweet or savory breakfast person, these bowls will change how you think about yogurt. Instead of serving the yogurt plain, I mix it with tahini, lemon juice, and earthy spices to create a rich and creamy base for the bowls. I top it off with tomatoes, crisp veggies, and herbs and scoop it up with pita for a fresh, delicious breakfast. The yogurt mixture is easy enough to prepare on weekday mornings, but it also keeps well for a few days in the fridge.

TAHINI YOGURT

1 cup whole milk Greek yogurt

¼ cup tahini

2 tablespoons fresh lemon juice

2 garlic cloves, grated

1 teaspoon ground cumin

1 teaspoon sea salt, plus more for sprinkling

½ teaspoon ground cardamom

1 to 2 tablespoons water, if necessary

TOPPINGS

10 cherry tomatoes, halved

2 Persian cucumbers, thinly sliced or diced

2 red radishes or 1 watermelon radish, thinly sliced

2 tablespoons crushed pistachios

Pinch of Aleppo pepper or red pepper flakes (optional)

Fresh mint leaves

Pita, for serving

Make the tahini yogurt: In a medium bowl, stir together the yogurt, tahini, lemon juice, garlic, cumin, salt, and cardamom. If the yogurt is too thick, thin with water, 1 tablespoon at a time.

Divide the tahini yogurt among four bowls and top with the tomatoes, cucumbers, radishes, pistachios, and pepper flakes, if using. Sprinkle with salt and top with fresh mint. Serve with pita.

SERVES 4 | GLUTEN-FREE: Use gluten-free pita. | VEGAN: Replace the tahini yogurt with homemade hummus (page 256).

Skillet Granola

I came up with this recipe one Saturday morning when my oven was broken. I was craving granola and nothing—not even that broken oven—was going to stop me from making it. Enter: this stovetop granola! It came out just as toasty and nutty as traditional granola, and it was so simple to stir together. Even now that my oven is back in action, this recipe is still one of my go-to breakfasts.

1 cup whole rolled oats

1 tablespoon coconut oil

1 teaspoon cinnamon

½ teaspoon sea salt

1 cup chopped walnuts

3 tablespoons maple syrup

SERVING SUGGESTIONS

Yogurt or vegan yogurt

Fresh fruit

Dried fruit

Other nuts or seeds

Place the oats in a medium skillet over low heat and let them toast, stirring occasionally, for 2 minutes. Add the coconut oil, cinnamon, and salt and cook, stirring occasionally, for 3 minutes. Add the walnuts and maple syrup. Stir to coat and cook for 7 to 8 minutes, stirring often and reducing the heat as needed so that the mixture doesn't burn. Remove the pan from the heat and set aside for 15 minutes to allow the granola to crisp up. It'll still be a little soft but will get crisp as it cools.

Serve with yogurt and desired toppings.

SERVES 4 | **GLUTEN-FREE:** Use certified gluten-free oats. | **VEGAN**

Southwestern Veggie Hash

I lived in Austin for many years, so my favorite type of breakfast is one that has salsa or hot sauce on the side. These little veggie skillets are so quick and easy to put together, even on a weekday. If you're vegan, skip the fried eggs and top them with sliced avocado instead.

2½ teaspoons extra-virgin olive oil

4 large eggs

1 red bell pepper, stemmed, seeded, and chopped

1 small zucchini, chopped

¾ cup cooked black beans, drained and rinsed (page 72)

½ cup corn kernels, fresh or frozen

½ cup chopped scallions

1¼ teaspoons chili powder

¾ teaspoon sea salt

1 tablespoon fresh lime juice

Fresh cilantro, for serving (optional)

Pickled Onions, for serving (page 78, optional)

Hot sauce or salsa, for serving (optional)

Tortilla chips, for serving (optional)

Freshly ground black pepper

Heat ½ teaspoon of the olive oil in a large nonstick or cast-iron skillet over medium heat. Add the eggs, reduce the heat to low, and cook, covered, for 2 to 3 minutes, or until the yolks are just set. Remove the eggs from the pan and set aside. Cover loosely with foil if you'd like to keep them hot while you sauté the veggies.

Heat the remaining 2 teaspoons olive oil in the pan over medium heat. Add the bell pepper, zucchini, black beans, corn, scallions, chili powder, salt, and several grinds of pepper. Sauté for 6 to 8 minutes, or until tender. Stir in the lime juice and season to taste.

Divide the hash among four plates. Top with the fried eggs and serve with cilantro, pickled onions, hot sauce, and tortilla chips, if desired.

SERVES 4 | **GLUTEN-FREE** | **VEGAN:** Skip the eggs and top with sliced avocado instead.

Spiced Chickpea Waffles

If you ever crave falafel in the morning, these waffles are for you! Made with chickpea flour, fresh herbs, and spices, they're hearty, flavorful, and filled with plant-based protein. They're best when they're very crisp, so be sure not to undercook them—I typically give them a minute or two longer than regular waffles.

2½ cups chickpea flour, spooned and leveled (see page 23)

1 teaspoon baking powder

1 teaspoon ground coriander

1 teaspoon ground cumin

1 teaspoon sea salt

½ teaspoon cayenne pepper (optional)

1½ cups water

¾ cup extra-virgin olive oil

¼ cup chopped fresh cilantro, plus more for garnish

4 scallions, chopped

2 garlic cloves, grated

Freshly ground black pepper

TOPPING SUGGESTIONS

Tahini Yogurt (page 257) or Tahini Sauce (page 256)

Pickled Onions (page 78)

Diced cucumber

Diced tomato

Fresh mint or cilantro leaves

Preheat a waffle iron and prepare your desired toppings.

In a large bowl, whisk together the chickpea flour, baking powder, coriander, cumin, salt, cayenne, if using, and several grinds of pepper. Add the water, olive oil, cilantro, scallions, and garlic and stir until combined.

Scoop ½ cup of batter for each waffle into a large Belgian waffle maker, or scoop an appropriate amount for your waffle maker. Cook for 4 to 9 minutes, or until golden brown and lightly crisp. The timing will depend on your waffle iron. I like to cook these savory waffles longer than sweet waffles to get them crisper.

Serve with desired toppings.

SERVES 6 | GLUTEN-FREE | **VEGAN:** Serve with tahini sauce (page 256) instead of tahini yogurt.

SHAKING UP
SHAKSHUKA

BASIC RECIPE

2 tablespoons extra-virgin olive oil

2 shallots, chopped (⅔ cup)

1 teaspoon whole cumin seeds

1 (28-ounce) can crushed fire-roasted tomatoes

1 cup chopped jarred roasted red peppers

3 garlic cloves, grated

½ teaspoon sea salt, plus more to taste

4 to 6 large eggs

¼ cup fresh parsley leaves

¼ cup crumbled feta cheese or ½ avocado, sliced

Pita, for serving

Freshly ground black pepper

1. Heat the olive oil in a large, lidded skillet over medium heat. Add the shallots and cook until soft, about 4 minutes. Add the cumin seeds and cook for 2 more minutes.

2. Add the tomatoes, red peppers, garlic, salt, and several grinds of pepper. Simmer over low heat, stirring often, for 15 minutes, or until the sauce has thickened.

3. Make 4 to 6 wells in the sauce and crack one egg into each well. Cover and cook for 4 to 8 minutes, or until the eggs are set. The timing will depend on how runny or firm you like your eggs.

4. Season with salt and pepper and top with the parsley and feta or avocado. Serve with pita.

SERVES 4

CHICKPEA & KALE SHAKSHUKA

1½ cups cooked chickpeas, drained and rinsed (page 72)

4 kale leaves, stemmed, leaves torn

¼ cup fresh cilantro leaves

Follow the basic recipe, adding the chickpeas to the skillet in Step 2 along with the tomatoes. Once the sauce has thickened, stir in the kale leaves and cook for 2 minutes, or until wilted, then move on to Step 3. Use cilantro instead of parsley in Step 4.

VEGAN: Skip the eggs.

SMOKY EGGPLANT SHAKSHUKA

Roasted Eggplant (page 161)

½ teaspoon smoked paprika

Tahini Yogurt (page 257)

¼ cup fresh mint leaves

Follow the basic recipe, omitting the cumin seeds and adding the roasted eggplant and smoked paprika to the skillet in Step 2 along with the tomatoes. Serve with dollops of tahini yogurt instead of the feta or avocado and sprinkle with mint instead of parsley in Step 4.

BURST CHERRY TOMATO & BASIL SHAKSHUKA

1 (14-ounce) can crushed tomatoes

2 pints cherry tomatoes

Zest of 1 lemon

¼ cup fresh basil leaves

1 tablespoon chopped fresh dill

Follow the basic recipe, omitting the cumin seeds and using the 14-ounce can of regular crushed tomatoes instead of the 28-ounce can of fire-roasted tomatoes. Add 1 pint of the cherry tomatoes and the lemon zest to the skillet in Step 2 along with the canned tomatoes. Add the remaining cherry tomatoes to the skillet halfway through the cooking time in Step 2. Use basil and dill instead of parsley in Step 4 and omit the feta or avocado.

Curried Lentil Freezer Burritos

Instead of using traditional fillings in these freezer breakfast burritos, I stuff them with spiced red lentils, chewy brown rice, kale, and crisp veggies. These ingredients freeze and thaw perfectly for grab-and-go breakfasts all week long. The mint chutney kicks the flavors up a notch, but a few squeezes of lime will do the trick in a pinch.

1½ teaspoons coconut oil

½ medium white onion, chopped

1 cup dry red lentils, rinsed

2 garlic cloves, grated

1 teaspoon sea salt

½ teaspoon grated fresh ginger

½ teaspoon ground cumin

¼ teaspoon ground cardamom

¼ teaspoon ground coriander

¼ teaspoon ground turmeric

2 cups water

1 tablespoon fresh lime juice

6 (10-inch) flour tortillas

FILLING & SERVING OPTIONS

1½ cups cooked brown rice (page 71)

2 medium kale leaves, stemmed, leaves torn

¼ medium white onion, diced

½ green bell pepper, stemmed, seeded, and diced

½ cup fresh cilantro, finely chopped

Mint Chutney (page 256) or lime wedges, for serving

Heat the coconut oil in a medium pot over medium heat. Add the onion and a pinch of salt and cook, stirring, for 5 to 8 minutes, or until soft and browned. Add the lentils, garlic, salt, ginger, cumin, cardamom, coriander, and turmeric and cook for 30 seconds, or until fragrant. Add the water and bring to a boil. Reduce the heat and simmer, covered, for 15 to 20 minutes, or until the lentils are tender. Stir in the lime juice and set aside to cool and thicken for 30 minutes. Meanwhile, prep the other fillings.

Fill each tortilla with ½ cup of the lentil mixture, ¼ cup of the rice, and some of the kale, onion, bell pepper, and cilantro. Fold the left and right sides of the tortilla over the filling. Fold the bottom flap of the tortilla up and over the filling and roll the burrito closed, tucking the sides around the filling as you roll.

Serve with mint chutney. Enjoy the burritos freshly made or wrap in foil and freeze for later.

Transfer frozen burritos to the fridge to thaw overnight, or unwrap and defrost in the microwave.

SERVES 6 | **GLUTEN-FREE:** Use gluten-free tortillas. | **VEGAN**

Butternut Squash & Feta Muffins

This recipe is autumn in a muffin. Lightly sweet roasted squash and a little bit of maple syrup contrast perfectly with savory scallions, rosemary, feta, and crispy pepitas. Pair these muffins with visions of falling leaves and a slight chill in the air for the ultimate feel-good breakfast.

3 cups peeled and cubed butternut squash (¼-inch cubes)

⅓ cup plus 1 teaspoon extra-virgin olive oil

2 large eggs

1 cup unsweetened almond milk

¼ cup maple syrup

1 tablespoon apple cider vinegar

1 cup all-purpose flour, spooned and leveled (see page 23)

¾ cup whole wheat flour, spooned and leveled (see page 23)

1 teaspoon baking powder

1 teaspoon sea salt

½ teaspoon baking soda

¼ teaspoon cinnamon

½ cup chopped scallions

½ cup crumbled feta cheese

1½ tablespoons minced fresh rosemary

¼ cup pepitas

Freshly ground black pepper

Preheat the oven to 425°F and line a baking sheet with parchment paper.

Place the squash on the baking sheet and drizzle with 1 teaspoon of the olive oil. Toss to coat and spread evenly on the baking sheet. Roast for 25 minutes, or until soft.

Reduce the oven temperature to 350°F and lightly oil or spray a 12-cup muffin tin.

Measure ½ cup of the squash cubes and set aside. Put the remaining squash in a large bowl and mash well. Add the remaining ⅓ cup olive oil, the eggs, almond milk, maple syrup, and vinegar and whisk until combined.

In a medium bowl, whisk together the all-purpose and whole wheat flours, the baking powder, salt, baking soda, cinnamon, and several grinds of pepper.

Add the dry ingredients to the wet ingredients and stir until just combined. Fold in the scallions, feta, rosemary, and the reserved ½ cup roasted squash.

Divide the batter evenly into the muffin tin, sprinkle with the pepitas, and bake for 20 to 22 minutes, or until a toothpick inserted in the center comes out clean.

Let cool for 10 minutes, then remove from the pan and place on a wire rack to finish cooling.

Store in an airtight container at room temperature for 1 to 2 days or freeze for up to 3 months.

MAKES 12 MUFFINS

Carrot Cake Smoothies

Seriously—who wouldn't like to eat carrot cake for breakfast? Creamy, tangy, and warmly spiced, this smoothie is nearly dessert in a glass. It may be a little more involved than the average smoothie, but it's totally worth it—and very doable—if you prep four servings in advance.

FREEZER PREP FOR 4 SMOOTHIES

8 medium carrots, peeled and cut into ½-inch pieces

1 medium sweet potato, peeled and cut into ½-inch pieces

Melted coconut oil, for drizzling

2 cups frozen pineapple

¾ cup chopped pecans

2 tablespoons chia seeds

4 teaspoons cinnamon

2 teaspoons ground ginger

1 teaspoon nutmeg

REMAINING INGREDIENTS FOR EACH SMOOTHIE

3 soft Medjool dates, pitted

1¼ cups almond milk, plus more as needed

¼ teaspoon vanilla extract

Pinch of sea salt

4 ice cubes

Preheat the oven to 425°F and line two baking sheets with parchment paper.

Place the carrots and sweet potato on one of the baking sheets and drizzle with coconut oil. Toss to coat and spread evenly on the baking sheet. Cover with foil and bake for 30 to 40 minutes, or until the vegetables are soft.

Let cool, then spread onto the second prepared baking sheet. Freeze for 1 hour, then divide into four freezer-safe containers. Evenly divide the frozen pineapple, pecans, chia seeds, cinnamon, ginger, and nutmeg among the containers and freeze until ready to use.

Make one smoothie: If your dates are not soft, soak them in a small bowl of warm water for 5 to 10 minutes.

In a blender, place one container of the carrots and sweet potatoes, the soft dates, almond milk, vanilla, and salt. Blend until smooth, adding more almond milk as needed to blend. Add the ice and blend again.

SERVES 1 *with prep for 3 additional smoothies* | GLUTEN-FREE | VEGAN

*It's easiest to work with the coconut oil for this recipe if you measure it while it's soft. Then, place it in a small bowl and freeze for 15 minutes. Use a paring knife to cut it into small pieces.

Lemon Cornmeal Scones

If I could choose one treat to have in my freezer all the time, I'd pick these scones. They're wholesome and delicious, and the zesty glaze gives them an irresistible pop of bright citrus flavor. Even with the glaze, they freeze and thaw perfectly.

2 large eggs

¼ cup almond milk

3 tablespoons fresh lemon juice

2 tablespoons lemon zest

1 cup all-purpose flour, spooned and leveled, plus more for kneading (see page 23)

1 cup whole wheat flour, spooned and leveled (see page 23)

¾ cup cornmeal, spooned and leveled (see page 23)

⅓ cup cane sugar

2½ teaspoons baking powder

¾ teaspoon sea salt

½ cup coconut oil, hardened and cut into small pieces*

GLAZE & ZEST TOPPING

1 cup powdered sugar

2 to 3 tablespoons fresh lemon juice

1 teaspoon lemon zest

In a medium bowl, whisk together the eggs, almond milk, and lemon juice and zest.

In a food processor, place the all-purpose and whole wheat flours, the cornmeal, sugar, baking powder, and salt and pulse several times to combine. Add the hardened coconut oil and pulse a few times until just combined. Add the egg mixture and process until the dough just comes together. Be careful not to overmix.

Remove the dough from the food processor and place on a floured surface. Knead lightly, using more flour as needed to prevent sticking. Form the dough into a ball, divide it in half, and flatten each half into a 1-inch-thick disk. Place on a parchment paper–lined baking sheet and freeze for 20 minutes.

Preheat the oven to 400°F and line another baking sheet with parchment paper.

Remove the dough from the freezer and cut each disk into 6 wedges. Separate the wedges and arrange them on the prepared baking sheet. Bake for 15 to 17 minutes, or until golden brown around the edges. Transfer to a wire rack to cool.

Make the glaze and zest topping: In a medium bowl, whisk together the powdered sugar and lemon juice until smooth. Drizzle over the cooled scones and sprinkle with the zest.

Store in an airtight container at room temperature for 1 to 2 days or freeze for up to 3 months.

MAKES 12 SCONES

VEGAN: Mix 2 tablespoons ground flaxseed with 5 tablespoons water. Let thicken for 5 minutes, then add to the recipe in place of the eggs. Increase the baking powder to 1 tablespoon.

PANCAKE MIX

PANCAKE DRY MIX

1½ cups all-purpose flour, spooned and leveled (see page 23)

2 tablespoons cane sugar

2 teaspoons baking powder

Heaping 1 teaspoon cinnamon

½ teaspoon baking soda

Heaping ¼ teaspoon sea salt

PLAIN PANCAKES
WET INGREDIENTS

1 large egg

1 cup plus 3 tablespoons almond milk

½ cup whole milk Greek yogurt

2 tablespoons avocado oil, plus more for brushing

1½ teaspoons vanilla extract

Maple syrup, for serving

VEGAN:

In a small bowl, mix 1 tablespoon ground flaxseed with 3 tablespoons water. Set aside for 5 minutes to thicken, then use in the pancakes in place of the egg. Use applesauce instead of the Greek yogurt, or use the listed alternative for your variation.

MAKES 10 TO 12 PANCAKES

*Get ahead by making the pancake dry mix in advance!
Cover it and store it in a cool, dry place until
you're ready to make pancakes.*

＋ MIX-INS

To make pancakes: Choose a variation. In a large bowl, whisk together the pancake dry mix and any additional dry ingredients. In a medium bowl, whisk together the plain pancakes wet ingredients and any additional wet ingredients. Add the wet ingredients to the dry ingredients and mix until just combined. Fold in any mix-ins. Heat a nonstick skillet over medium-low heat and brush lightly with oil. Use a ⅓-cup scoop to pour the batter into the skillet. Cook the pancakes for 1 to 4 minutes per side. Serve with maple syrup or specified toppings.

PB&J PANCAKES

Replace the Greek yogurt with ½ cup mashed banana and add 2 tablespoons creamy peanut butter to the wet ingredients. Serve with strawberry jam.

PUMPKIN CHOCOLATE CHIP PANCAKES

Whisk 2 teaspoons pumpkin pie spice into the pancake dry mix. Replace the Greek yogurt with ½ cup pumpkin puree. Fold in ½ cup dark chocolate chips.

APPLE GINGERBREAD PANCAKES

Whisk ½ teaspoon ground ginger and ¼ teaspoon ground cardamom into the pancake dry mix. Replace the Greek yogurt with ½ cup applesauce and add 2 tablespoons molasses to the wet ingredients. Fold in ½ cup diced apple.

RASPBERRY LEMON PANCAKES

Add 1 tablespoon fresh lemon juice and 1 tablespoon lemon zest to the wet ingredients. Fold in 1 cup raspberries, halved if large, and 1 teaspoon poppy seeds.

PEAR HAZELNUT COFFEE CAKE PANCAKES

Fold in ½ cup diced pear.

Make a crumble topping: In a skillet over low heat, toast 1 cup rolled oats and ¼ cup hazelnuts for 2 minutes. Transfer to a food processor and add ¼ cup almond flour, 2 tablespoons brown sugar, ½ teaspoon cinnamon, and ⅛ teaspoon salt. Pulse until combined. Add ¼ cup coconut oil and pulse until crumbly. Serve over the pancakes with maple syrup.

Salads

TIP

Wait till summer to make this salad! Because it's so simple, you'll really be able to taste the difference between peak-season tomatoes and out-of-season ones.

Sesame Heirloom Tomato Salad

I frequent the farmers market as if it's my church—every Sunday. And every week in the summer, I bring home as many colorful heirloom tomatoes as I can carry. It would be sacrilege to cover up their beauty with a complicated recipe. Instead, I use simple yet unexpected ingredients—lime juice, sesame oil, and a toasted seed topping—to highlight their vibrant flavor.

2 tablespoons pepitas

2 tablespoons raw, hulled sunflower seeds

2 tablespoons sesame seeds

1 teaspoon tamari

2 pounds colorful heirloom tomatoes, sliced

1 avocado, thinly sliced

2 scallions, thinly sliced

2 teaspoons fresh lime juice

1 teaspoon toasted sesame oil

Flaky sea salt

Microgreens, for garnish

Preheat the oven to 350°F and line a baking sheet with parchment paper.

Place the pepitas, sunflower seeds, and sesame seeds on the baking sheet, toss with the tamari, and spread evenly on the baking sheet. Bake for 7 to 10 minutes, or until golden brown and toasty. Remove from the oven and let cool for 5 minutes to allow the seeds to crisp up.

Arrange the tomatoes on a large platter in a single layer, overlapping only slightly. Top with the avocado slices and scallions and drizzle with the lime juice and sesame oil. Sprinkle with flaky sea salt, the seed topping, and microgreens and serve.

SERVES 4　　　　**GLUTEN-FREE:** Use certified gluten-free tamari.　　|　**VEGAN**

Beautiful Root Veggie Salad

If you invite me over for dinner and ask me to bring a salad, you'd better bet that I'll go out of my way to bring a super-beautiful one. But beautiful must also be delicious. The first time I made this salad, I served it to my family at a Christmas dinner. Even my meat-eating dad asked, "Can I have more of THAT salad??"

1 tablespoon extra-virgin olive oil

1 tablespoon fresh lemon juice

½ teaspoon honey

½ teaspoon sea salt

1 golden beet, peeled and thinly sliced on a mandoline

1 watermelon radish, thinly sliced on a mandoline

Tahini Yogurt (page 257)

4 rainbow carrots, peeled into ribbons

1 parsnip, peeled into ribbons

2 tablespoons finely chopped fresh parsley

1 pear, thinly sliced

2 tablespoons chopped toasted hazelnuts, walnuts, or pecans (page 78)

Freshly ground black pepper

In a large bowl, whisk together the olive oil, lemon juice, honey, salt, and several grinds of pepper. Add the beet and radish slices, toss to coat, and set aside for 15 minutes to soften.

Spread the tahini yogurt on a shallow serving platter.

Add the carrot and parsnip ribbons and the parsley to the bowl with the vegetables and toss to coat.

Arrange the vegetables on the serving platter on top of the tahini yogurt. Layer the pear slices evenly on the vegetables, top with the nuts, and serve.

SERVES 4

GLUTEN-FREE

Lemony Celery Chickpea Salad

If you have fresh farmers market celery—the kind with big, beautiful leaves attached—you need to make this salad. If you have ordinary grocery store celery—the kind that generally impresses no one—you still need to make this salad. This crunchy, herby one-bowl salad is far more than the sum of its parts. Easy and delicious, it's perfect for picnics and lunches.

¼ cup extra-virgin olive oil

¼ cup fresh lemon juice

2 small garlic cloves, grated

2 teaspoons Dijon mustard

1 teaspoon sea salt

3 cups cooked chickpeas, drained and rinsed (page 72)

8 large celery stalks with leaves, stalks sliced on the bias, leaves chopped

⅔ cup thinly sliced red onion

¼ cup chopped fresh dill

Freshly ground black pepper

In a large bowl, whisk together the olive oil, lemon juice, garlic, mustard, salt, and several grinds of pepper.

Add the chickpeas, celery stalks and leaves, onion, and dill and toss to combine. Season to taste and serve.

SERVES 4 TO 6

GLUTEN-FREE | VEGAN

TIP

Add cooked farro
or wheat berries
(page 70) to make
this salad heartier.

Roasted Broccoli Salad with Curry Vinaigrette

One of our favorite lunch spots in Chicago is this healthy veggie restaurant called Left Coast. One day, they added a salad with the most delicious creamy curry vinaigrette. I was surprised to learn that its rich and creamy texture didn't come from yogurt or coconut milk, but from blended and emulsified dates. I started to worry that they'd take it off the menu—it was that good! So, to calm my fears, I re-created the dressing at home. I love the punchy vinaigrette on almost any salad or grain bowl, but it really shines against the sweet and nutty flavors in this roasted broccoli salad.

Florets from 2 broccoli crowns

Extra-virgin olive oil, for drizzling

3 soft Medjool dates, pitted

4 cups loose-packed fresh spinach

½ large pear, sliced into thin strips

Curry Vinaigrette (page 76)

¼ cup toasted pepitas or chopped pistachios (page 78)

Sea salt and freshly ground black pepper

Preheat the oven to 400°F and line a baking sheet with parchment paper.

Place the broccoli florets on the baking sheet, drizzle with olive oil, and season with salt and pepper. Toss to coat and spread evenly on the baking sheet. Roast for 15 to 20 minutes, or until browned around the edges.

If your dates are not soft, soak them in a small bowl of warm water for 5 to 10 minutes. Pat dry and chop before adding to the salad.

Assemble the salad on a platter with the dates, spinach, pear, and generous drizzles of the vinaigrette. Add the broccoli, half the pepitas, and another drizzle of dressing. I like to use just over half of the total amount of dressing for this salad. Top with the remaining pepitas. Season to taste and serve.

SERVES 4

GLUTEN-FREE | VEGAN

ONE DRESSING, 5 SIMPLE SALADS

1
BITTER GREENS

2
SUMMER CORN & PEACH

BASIC LEMON DRESSING

¼ cup extra-virgin olive oil

¼ cup fresh lemon juice

1 small garlic clove, grated

1 teaspoon Dijon mustard

½ teaspoon honey or maple syrup

¼ teaspoon sea salt

Freshly ground black pepper

In a small lidded jar, place the olive oil, lemon juice, garlic, mustard, honey, salt, and several grinds of pepper. Cover and shake to combine.

6 cups arugula

1½ cups thinly sliced radicchio

¼ cup golden raisins

⅓ cup shaved pecorino cheese

3 tablespoons pine nuts

⅓ cup thinly sliced red onion

Kernels from 4 ears corn

1 avocado, chopped

1 peach, chopped

½ cup fresh cilantro leaves

Choose a variation. Place the ingredients in a large bowl and toss to combine. Drizzle with some of the dressing and toss again. Season with ¼ teaspoon sea salt, plus more to taste, and freshly ground black pepper and serve.

3

SPRINGY
ASPARAGUS

2 bunches asparagus, blanched
and chopped into 1-inch pieces

1 cup frozen peas, thawed

4 thinly sliced red radishes

⅓ cup crumbled feta cheese

3 tablespoons chopped fresh dill

4

FENNEL
CITRUS

2 fennel bulbs,
very thinly sliced

Segments from ½ grapefruit

Segments from ½ orange

¼ cup chopped pistachios

⅓ cup fresh mint leaves

5

LITTLE GEM
STRAWBERRY

1 shallot, thinly sliced

6 ounces Little Gem lettuce

3 cups sliced strawberries

3 ounces goat cheese

½ cup chopped walnuts

Wild Rice Harvest Salad

This harvest salad serves two purposes. Because it's so pretty,
it's a perfect side dish for any fall gathering—even Thanksgiving!
And because its hearty ingredients keep well in the fridge for a
few days without wilting, it's also a great salad to pack for lunch.

1 tablespoon extra-virgin olive oil

10 ounces cremini mushrooms, stemmed and sliced

1 shallot, chopped (⅓ cup)

½ teaspoon sea salt, plus more to taste

1 tablespoon fresh thyme leaves

2 cups cooked and cooled wild rice/brown rice blend (page 257)

8 ounces Brussels sprouts, very thinly sliced

2 celery stalks, chopped

½ cup dried cranberries

¼ cup chopped toasted pecans (page 78)

1 apple, diced

2 ounces goat cheese

Freshly ground black pepper

DRESSING

¼ cup extra-virgin olive oil

¼ cup apple cider vinegar

1 garlic clove, grated

½ teaspoon sea salt

¼ teaspoon Dijon mustard

Freshly ground black pepper

Heat the olive oil in a medium skillet over medium heat. Add the mushrooms, shallot, salt, and several grinds of pepper and toss to coat. Let the mushrooms cook, without stirring, for 2 minutes. Stir, and then continue cooking, stirring occasionally, until the mushrooms are soft and well browned, about 5 more minutes. Stir in the thyme. Transfer the mushroom mixture to a plate and set aside.

Make the dressing: In a small lidded jar, combine the olive oil, vinegar, garlic, salt, mustard, and several grinds of pepper and shake well.

In a large bowl, assemble the salad with the rice, mushrooms, Brussels sprouts, celery, cranberries, pecans, and apple. Drizzle with half the dressing and toss. Dot with the goat cheese.

If you're preparing this salad in advance, portion it into meal prep containers and refrigerate for up to 3 days.

When ready to serve, drizzle with more dressing and season with salt and pepper to taste. If you're making it more than 2 days in advance, wait to add the apple until right before you eat.

SERVES 4 | **GLUTEN-FREE** | **VEGAN:** Skip the cheese.

Lentil Salad with Green Tahini

I'll never get tired of eating this salad for lunch—lemony lentils and crisp veggies doused in a creamy green dressing. But I don't make it the exact same way every time. Instead, I play around with the herbs in the dressing. I might use parsley instead of cilantro or experiment with adding tarragon, dill, or chives. I love that it's a little bit different each time I eat it!

6 ounces snap peas

1 shallot, finely chopped (⅓ cup)

3 tablespoons fresh lemon juice

1 tablespoon extra-virgin olive oil

1 teaspoon sea salt

3 cups cooked green lentils (page 72)

2 Persian cucumbers, diced

1 watermelon radish, sliced paper thin, or ½ cup daikon radish slices

Green Tahini, for serving (page 77)

Fresh mint leaves, for garnish

Freshly ground black pepper

Bring a large pot of salted water to a boil and set a bowl of ice water nearby. Drop the snap peas into the boiling water and blanch for 1 to 2 minutes, or until tender but still bright green. Use a slotted spoon to scoop the snap peas out of the boiling water and into the ice water. Chill for 1 minute, then drain and transfer to a kitchen towel to dry. Chop into 1-inch pieces and set aside.

In a large bowl, whisk together the shallot, lemon juice, olive oil, salt, and several grinds of pepper. Add the lentils and toss to coat. Transfer to a serving platter or meal prep containers and top with the snap peas, cucumbers, and radish slices.

When ready to serve, drizzle with the green tahini and garnish with mint leaves.

SERVES 4 TO 6

GLUTEN-FREE | VEGAN

NOTE:

If you're preparing this salad in advance, portion it into meal prep containers and refrigerate for up to 3 days. Store the peanuts separately at room temperature so that they retain their crunch, and wait to add the herbs until right before you eat.

Coconut Slaw with Spicy Peanuts

No wilted greens here! This crisp cabbage and bok choy slaw doesn't just hold up well to its creamy dressing; its texture and flavor actually improve as it sits in the fridge. Pack it up for a picnic, or make it ahead for a refreshing weekday lunch.

14 ounces extra-firm tofu, patted dry and cut into ½-inch cubes

Melted coconut oil, for drizzling

Sriracha, for drizzling

½ cup unsalted peanuts, chopped

½ cup full-fat coconut milk

¼ cup creamy peanut butter

Juice and zest of 1 lime, plus wedges for serving

2 garlic cloves, grated

2 teaspoons grated fresh ginger

6 cups shredded red cabbage

2 baby bok choy, thinly sliced horizontally (4 cups)

1 red bell pepper, stemmed, seeded, and thinly sliced

1 bunch scallions, chopped

½ cup fresh basil leaves, torn

½ cup fresh mint leaves

Sea salt

Preheat the oven to 425°F and line two baking sheets with parchment paper.

Place the tofu on one of the baking sheets, sprinkle with ½ teaspoon salt, drizzle with coconut oil and sriracha, toss, and spread evenly on the baking sheet. Place the peanuts on the second baking sheet, sprinkle with ½ teaspoon salt, drizzle with coconut oil and sriracha, toss, and spread evenly on the baking sheet. Roast the peanuts for 7 minutes. Roast the tofu for 25 to 30 minutes, or until golden brown.

In a medium bowl, whisk together the coconut milk, peanut butter, lime juice and zest, garlic, ginger, and a heaping ½ teaspoon salt.

In a very large bowl, combine the cabbage, bok choy, bell pepper, and scallions and toss. Add two-thirds of the dressing and ¼ teaspoon salt and toss to coat. Set aside for 10 minutes.

Top with the tofu and peanuts and garnish with the basil and mint. Season to taste and serve with lime wedges and the remaining dressing on the side.

SERVES 4 TO 6

GLUTEN-FREE | VEGAN

TIP

Soba noodles are made with buckwheat flour, which gives them a tendency to clump together when they're cooked. To prevent clumping, rinse them under cool water after you drain them. To save a pot in this recipe, cook the noodles in the same water you use to blanch the green beans.

Green Bean Tempeh Soba Salad

When I meal prep this salad for lunch, I spend all morning counting down the minutes until I get to eat it. It's insanely flavorful and super satisfying, thanks to the gooey noodles, crisp green beans, and nutty tempeh. If you're new to cooking tempeh, the trick to preparing it well is to steam it first. The hot steam helps it become more tender, which in turn helps it soak up the bold, punchy flavors in this recipe.

DRESSING

¼ cup plus 2 tablespoons rice vinegar
¼ cup plus 2 tablespoons tamari
¼ cup fresh lime juice
3 tablespoons toasted sesame oil
1½ tablespoons honey or maple syrup
1 tablespoon grated fresh ginger

FOR THE SALAD

8 ounces steamed tempeh (page 73)
12 ounces fresh green beans
8 ounces soba noodles, cooked
¾ cup frozen edamame, thawed
½ cup kimchi
1 tablespoon sesame seeds
2 or 3 sliced Thai chiles (optional)

Preheat the oven to 425°F and line a baking sheet with parchment paper.

Make the dressing: In a lidded jar, place the rice vinegar, tamari, lime juice, sesame oil, honey, and ginger. Shake well to combine.

Place the steamed tempeh on the baking sheet, toss with 1 tablespoon of the dressing, and spread evenly on the baking sheet. Roast for 20 minutes, or until lightly golden brown around the edges. Remove from the oven and toss with 2 more tablespoons of the dressing.

Bring a large pot of water to a boil and set a large bowl of ice water nearby. Drop the green beans into the boiling water and blanch for 3 minutes, or until tender but still bright green. Use a slotted spoon to scoop the green beans out of the boiling water and into the ice water. Chill for 1 minute, then drain and transfer to a kitchen towel to dry.

Place the soba noodles in the empty ice water bowl and toss with ¼ cup of the dressing.

Portion the noodles into bowls or meal prep containers. Assemble the salads with the green beans, tempeh, edamame, and kimchi. Lightly drizzle with the dressing. Top with the sesame seeds and Thai chiles, if using. If you're preparing this salad in advance, refrigerate for up to 3 days.

Serve with the remaining dressing on the side.

SERVES 4 TO 6 | **GLUTEN-FREE:** Use certified gluten-free tamari and 100% buckwheat soba noodles. | **VEGAN:** Use vegan kimchi.

GRAIN

MIX THESE >>

VEGGIE + GRAIN

1.   sautéed broccolini   wheat berries

2.   roasted radishes   bulgur

3.   sautéed bok choy   black rice

4.   sautéed snow peas   brown rice

5.   roasted sweet potato   quinoa

6.   roasted Brussels sprouts   basmati rice

7.   roasted carrots   millet

8.   roasted cauliflower   farro

BOWLS

PROTEIN + SAUCE   *Extras*

Protein		Sauce		Extras
lentils		green tahini		peas, pickled onion, preserved lemons, mint
roasted chickpeas		tahini yogurt		cucumbers, pistachios, dill, feta, mint, massaged kale
soft-boiled egg		cashew gochujang		chopped cashews, kimchi
edamame		miso citrus dressing		avocado, pickled ginger, sesame seeds, microgreens
black beans		creamy tomatillo sauce		cilantro, pepitas, pickled onion, sliced jalapeño
baked tofu		curry vinaigrette		chopped peanuts, sriracha, mint
smoky tempeh		vegan ranch		salad greens, pickled cabbage, toasted sunflower seeds
white beans		chickpea romesco		arugula, olives, chopped almonds, drizzle of olive oil

ROASTED VEGETABLES

(CHOOSE ONE VEGETABLE)

1 pound Brussels sprouts, halved

1 pound carrots, cut into big chunks

1 medium cauliflower, broken into florets

1 bunch radishes, halved

2 medium sweet potatoes, cut into 1-inch chunks

FOR EACH:

Extra-virgin olive oil, for drizzling

Sea salt and freshly ground black pepper

. . . .

Preheat the oven to 425°F and line a baking sheet with parchment paper.

Place the vegetables on the baking sheet, drizzle with olive oil, and season with salt and pepper. Toss to coat and spread evenly on the sheet. Roast until the vegetables are tender and browned around the edges:

20 to 30 minutes for Brussels sprouts

20 to 25 minutes for carrots

25 to 35 minutes for cauliflower

10 to 20 minutes for radishes

25 to 30 minutes for sweet potatoes

SAUTÉED VEGETABLES

(CHOOSE ONE VEGETABLE)

4 baby bok choy, quartered lengthwise

1 bunch broccolini, trimmed and
halved lengthwise*

8 ounces snow peas*

FOR EACH:

2 teaspoons avocado oil

2 tablespoons water

Sea salt

. . . .

Heat the avocado oil in a lidded skillet over
medium heat. Add the vegetables and a pinch
of salt and toss. Cook, tossing occasionally,
for 2 minutes. Add the water, cover, reduce
the heat, and cook for 3 to 5 minutes, tossing
occasionally, or until tender and bright green.

*We like to blanch these veggies too! It's a
great method if you're meal prepping your
bowls and you plan to eat them cold. Bring a
large pot of salted water to a boil and set a
bowl of ice water nearby. Drop the vegetables
into the boiling water and blanch for 1 to
2 minutes, or until tender and bright green.
Transfer to the ice water to stop the cooking
process, then drain and pat dry.*

GRAINS

Start by rinsing the grains. Place the dry grains in a strainer that fits inside a bowl and rinse under cool water until the water in the bowl runs clear. Drain, and you're ready to cook!

BULGUR

1 cup dry + 1 cup water

Yield: 2½ cups cooked

Bring the water to a boil and stir in the bulgur. Cover, remove from the heat, and let sit for 10 to 15 minutes, until tender. Drain excess water. Fluff with a fork.

FARRO OR WHEAT BERRIES

1 cup dry + pot of water

Yield: 3 cups cooked

Bring the water to a boil. Add the grains, reduce the heat, and simmer, uncovered, until tender, 9 to 11 minutes for quick-cooking farro; 25 to 40 minutes for whole farro or soft wheat berries; and 45 to 60 minutes for hard wheat berries. Add more water if necessary as the grains cook. Drain.

MILLET

1 cup dry + 2 cups water

Yield: 3½ cups cooked

Bring to a boil. Cover, reduce the heat, and simmer for 15 minutes. Remove from the heat and let sit, covered, for 10 minutes. Fluff with a fork.

QUINOA	1 cup dry + 1¾ cups water Yield: 3 cups cooked	Bring to a boil. Cover, reduce the heat, and simmer for 15 minutes. Remove from the heat and let sit, covered, for 10 minutes. Fluff with a fork.
BLACK RICE	1 cup dry + 1¾ cups water + 1 teaspoon extra-virgin olive oil Yield: 3 cups cooked	Bring to a boil. Cover, reduce the heat, and simmer for 30 minutes. Remove from the heat and let sit, covered, for 10 minutes. Fluff with a fork.
SHORT-GRAIN BROWN RICE	1 cup dry + 2 cups water + 1 teaspoon extra-virgin olive oil Yield: 3 cups cooked	Bring to a boil. Cover, reduce the heat, and simmer for 45 minutes. Remove from the heat and let sit, covered, for 10 minutes. Fluff with a fork.
WHITE JASMINE OR BASMATI RICE	1 cup dry + 1½ cups water + 1 teaspoon extra-virgin olive oil Yield: 3 cups cooked	Bring to a boil. Cover, reduce the heat, and simmer for 15 minutes. Remove from the heat and let sit, covered, for 10 minutes. Fluff with a fork.

PROTEINS

COOKED CHICKPEAS OR BEANS (BLACK, PINTO, OR WHITE)

1 cup dry chickpeas or beans

Place the beans in a large bowl. Discard any stones or debris. Cover with 2 to 3 inches of water and soak at room temperature for 8 hours or overnight. Drain and rinse. Place the soaked beans in a large pot and cover with 2 inches of water. Bring to a boil. Reduce the heat and simmer, uncovered, stirring occasionally, for 45 minutes to 2 hours, or until tender. The timing will depend on the type and freshness of your beans.

YIELD: 3 CUPS COOKED

COOKED LENTILS OR ADZUKI BEANS

1 cup dry green or French green lentils or adzuki beans, rinsed

Place the lentils or adzuki beans in a medium pot of water. Bring to a boil. Reduce the heat and simmer, uncovered, stirring occasionally, for 17 to 20 minutes for lentils and 30 to 45 minutes for adzuki beans, or until tender but not mushy. Drain.

YIELD: 2¼ TO 3 CUPS COOKED

ROASTED CHICKPEAS

1½ cups cooked chickpeas, drained and rinsed
Extra-virgin olive oil, for drizzling
Sea salt

Preheat the oven to 425°F and line a baking sheet with parchment paper.

Spread the chickpeas on a kitchen towel and pat dry. Remove any loose skins.

Place the chickpeas on the baking sheet, drizzle with olive oil, and season with salt. Toss to coat and spread evenly on the baking sheet. Roast for 20 to 30 minutes, or until golden brown and crisp.

BAKED TOFU

14 ounces extra-firm tofu, patted dry and cubed
2 tablespoons tamari
1½ teaspoons avocado oil
½ teaspoon sriracha
1 tablespoon cornstarch

Preheat the oven to 425°F and line a baking sheet with parchment paper.

Place the tofu on the baking sheet, drizzle with the tamari, avocado oil, and sriracha, and sprinkle with the cornstarch. Toss to coat and spread evenly on the baking sheet. Bake for 20 to 25 minutes, or until browned around the edges.

STEAMED TEMPEH

8 ounces tempeh, cut into 1-inch cubes

Place the tempeh in a steamer basket and set over a pot filled with 1 inch of water. Bring the water to a simmer, cover, and steam for 10 minutes. Use to make the Smoky Tempeh below or the Green Bean Tempeh Soba Salad on page 65.

SMOKY TEMPEH

3 tablespoons tamari

1½ tablespoons maple syrup

1½ tablespoons rice vinegar

2 teaspoons avocado oil

Heaping ¼ teaspoon smoked paprika

8 ounces steamed tempeh (see above)

Freshly ground black pepper

Preheat the oven to 425°F and line a baking sheet with parchment paper.

In a medium bowl, whisk together the tamari, maple syrup, vinegar, avocado oil, smoked paprika, and several grinds of pepper. Add the steamed tempeh and toss to coat. Spread the tempeh evenly on the baking sheet, reserving the excess tamari mixture.

Bake for 20 minutes, or until the cubes are charred around the edges. Remove from the oven and toss with the reserved tamari mixture.

SOFT-BOILED EGGS

4 large eggs

Bring a medium pot of water to a gentle simmer. Using a slotted spoon, carefully lower the eggs into the water and simmer for 7 minutes. Drain and rinse under cold water.

Tap the bottom of each egg to crack the shell. Carefully slide a small spoon in and around each egg to loosen and remove it from the shell.

CASHEW
GOCHUJANG
SAUCE

CURRY
VINAIGRETTE

CREAMY
TOMATILLO
SAUCE

VEGAN
RANCH

TAHINI YOGURT

GREEN TAHINI

CHICKPEA
ROMESCO

MISO CITRUS
DRESSING

SAUCES

CASHEW GOCHUJANG SAUCE

½ cup raw cashews

¼ cup plus 2 tablespoons water

3 tablespoons rice vinegar

2 tablespoons gochujang

1 tablespoon maple syrup

In a high-speed blender, place the cashews, water, vinegar, gochujang, and maple syrup and blend until smooth.

YIELD: ABOUT 1 CUP

CHICKPEA ROMESCO

2 jarred roasted red peppers

¾ cup cooked chickpeas, drained and rinsed (page 72)

2 tablespoons extra-virgin olive oil

1 garlic clove

1 teaspoon red wine vinegar

¼ teaspoon sea salt

¼ teaspoon smoked paprika

Freshly ground black pepper

In a blender, place the red peppers, chickpeas, olive oil, garlic, vinegar, salt, smoked paprika, and several grinds of pepper and blend until creamy.

YIELD: ABOUT 1 CUP

CREAMY TOMATILLO SAUCE

½ cup jarred tomatillo salsa

½ cup raw cashews

¼ cup water

1 tablespoon fresh lime juice

½ cup fresh cilantro

Sea salt

In a high-speed blender, place the salsa, cashews, water, and lime juice and blend until smooth. Add the cilantro and pulse until the sauce is smooth but green flecks are still visible. Season to taste.

YIELD: ¼ CUP

CURRY VINAIGRETTE

2 soft Medjool dates, pitted

½ cup extra-virgin olive oil

¼ cup water, plus more as needed

2 tablespoons rice vinegar

1 teaspoon curry powder

1 garlic clove

½ teaspoon grated fresh ginger

¼ teaspoon sea salt

Freshly ground black pepper

If your dates are not soft, soak them in a small bowl of warm water for 5 to 10 minutes. Pat dry before adding to the dressing.

In a blender, place the dates, olive oil, water, rice vinegar, curry powder, garlic, ginger, salt, and several grinds of pepper. Blend until smooth and emulsified. If the dressing is too thick, blend in more water to reach a drizzleable consistency.

YIELD: 1 CUP

GREEN TAHINI

1½ cups fresh parsley or cilantro

½ cup tahini

¼ cup fresh lemon juice

¼ cup fresh tarragon, chives, dill, or mint

3 tablespoons extra-virgin olive oil

1 teaspoon honey or maple syrup

1 garlic clove

½ teaspoon sea salt

4 to 6 tablespoons water, plus more as needed

In a food processor, place the parsley, tahini, lemon juice, tarragon, olive oil, honey, garlic, salt, and 4 tablespoons of the water. Process until smooth. If the sauce is too thick, thin with more water to reach a drizzleable consistency.

YIELD: ABOUT 1⅓ CUPS

MISO CITRUS DRESSING

Juice of 1 orange (about 6 tablespoons)

¼ cup avocado oil

¼ cup rice vinegar

¼ cup white miso paste

2 tablespoons tamari

2 tablespoons toasted sesame oil

1 teaspoon grated fresh ginger

In a small bowl, whisk together the orange juice, avocado oil, vinegar, miso paste, tamari, sesame oil, and ginger.

YIELD: ABOUT 1 CUP

TAHINI YOGURT

1 cup whole milk Greek yogurt

¼ cup tahini

2 tablespoons fresh lemon juice

2 garlic cloves, grated

1 teaspoon ground cumin

1 teaspoon sea salt

½ teaspoon ground cardamom

1 to 4 tablespoons water, if necessary

In a medium bowl, stir together the yogurt, tahini, lemon juice, garlic, cumin, salt, and cardamom. If the yogurt is too thick, thin with water, 1 tablespoon at a time, to reach a drizzleable consistency.

YIELD: ABOUT 1½ CUPS

VEGAN RANCH

1 cup raw cashews

½ cup water

2 tablespoons avocado oil

2 tablespoons fresh lime juice

½ teaspoon garlic powder

½ teaspoon onion powder

½ teaspoon sea salt

¼ teaspoon dried dill

In a high-speed blender, place the cashews, water, avocado oil, lime juice, garlic powder, onion powder, salt, and dill. Blend until smooth.

YIELD: 1 CUP

Extras

MASSAGED KALE

1 bunch curly kale, stemmed, leaves torn

1 teaspoon fresh lemon juice

½ teaspoon extra-virgin olive oil

Sea salt

In a large bowl, massage the kale with the lemon juice, olive oil, and a few pinches of salt until soft and wilted.

PICKLED CABBAGE

¼ medium red cabbage, shredded (3½ cups)

½ cup thinly sliced red onion

1 cup apple cider vinegar

1 cup water

2 teaspoons sea salt

In a large lidded jar, place the cabbage, onion, vinegar, water, and salt. Cover, shake to combine, and chill overnight.

TOASTED NUTS AND SEEDS

Raw nuts or seeds (pepitas, sesame seeds, cashews, pine nuts, etc.)

Place nuts or seeds in a dry skillet over medium-low heat. Toast, stirring often, for 1 to 5 minutes, or until lightly browned and fragrant. The timing will depend on the size and type of the nut or seed.

PICKLED ONIONS

1 small red onion, thinly sliced

1 cup water

1 cup distilled white vinegar

2 tablespoons cane sugar

1 tablespoon sea salt

Place the onions in a lidded 16-ounce jar.

In a small saucepan over medium heat, heat the water, vinegar, sugar, and salt. Stir until the sugar and salt dissolve, about 1 minute. Pour over the onions.

Set aside to cool to room temperature, then cover and chill overnight.

QUICK PRESERVED LEMONS

2 thin-skinned organic Meyer lemons

1 tablespoon cane sugar

1½ teaspoons sea salt

Finely dice the lemons, including the peel. Remove the seeds as you dice. Place the lemons, sugar, and salt in a lidded jar. Cover and shake. Chill for at least 3 hours, preferably overnight.

PROTEIN
i.e., roasted chickpeas

EXTRAS
i.e., cucumbers,
pistachios, dill, mint,
feta, massaged kale

VEGGIE
i.e., roasted radishes

PLUS A
SQUEEZE OF
LEMON!

GRAIN
i.e., bulgur

ROASTED RADISH GRAIN BOWL
(page 66)

SAUCE
i.e., tahini yogurt

CHAPTER

3

SOUPS

SOUPS

Creamy Tahini Chickpea Soup

This soup is so simple that if you have a few cans of chickpeas in your pantry, you're already well on your way to making it! Blended chickpeas and tahini make it nice and creamy, while whole chickpeas and silky spinach give it some texture. I like to serve this soup how I serve my hummus—with generous drizzles of olive oil, a sprinkle of red pepper flakes, and plenty of pita for dipping.

2 tablespoons extra-virgin olive oil, plus more for serving

1 bunch scallions, chopped

¾ teaspoon sea salt, plus more to taste

4 cups vegetable broth

3 cups cooked chickpeas, drained and rinsed (page 72)

2 tablespoons tahini

2 cups fresh spinach

2 tablespoons chopped fresh dill

2 tablespoons fresh lemon juice, plus wedges for serving

Red pepper flakes

Pita, for serving

Freshly ground black pepper

Heat the olive oil in a large pot over medium heat. Add the scallions, salt, and several grinds of pepper and cook for 2 minutes, or until softened but still bright green. Add 3 cups of the broth and 1⅔ cups of the chickpeas and simmer, uncovered, for 15 minutes.

Combine the remaining 1 cup broth, the remaining 1⅓ cups chickpeas, and the tahini in a blender and blend until creamy. Stir into the soup pot and simmer over low heat for 2 minutes.

Add the spinach, dill, and lemon juice and stir until the spinach is wilted. Season to taste with salt and pepper.

Portion into bowls and top with a generous swirl of olive oil, a squeeze of lemon juice, and a sprinkle of red pepper flakes. Serve with pita.

SERVES 4 | **GLUTEN-FREE:** Serve with gluten-free pita. | **VEGAN**

I love the heat that the jalapeños add to this comforting stew.
But if you're sensitive to spice, feel free to scale it back.
Remove the seeds from the jalapeños, or use just one pepper instead of two.

Spicy Red Lentil Sweet Potato Stew

I love to eat soup for lunch, but it often leaves me hungry before dinnertime. Not this one! Hearty sweet potatoes and protein-packed red lentils make it a filling midday meal, and jalapeño, ginger, garlic, and lime give it a kick of flavor.

2 tablespoons coconut oil

1 medium yellow onion, chopped

2 jalapeño peppers, stemmed and diced

2 tablespoons finely chopped fresh ginger

2 garlic cloves, chopped

1½ teaspoons sea salt

Stems from 1 bunch cilantro, diced, leaves reserved for garnish

2 medium sweet potatoes, chopped

4 cups vegetable broth

1 cup dry red lentils, rinsed

3 tablespoons fresh lime juice

Naan, for serving (optional)

Freshly ground black pepper

Heat the coconut oil in a large pot over medium heat. Add the onion, jalapeños, ginger, garlic, salt, and several grinds of pepper and cook, stirring occasionally, for 5 to 8 minutes, or until softened. Add the cilantro stems and sweet potatoes. Stir and cook for 2 minutes. Add the broth and lentils, stir, and simmer, uncovered, for 30 minutes.

Stir the lime juice into the soup. Season to taste and garnish with the reserved cilantro leaves. Serve with naan, if desired.

SERVES 4 TO 6

GLUTEN-FREE | VEGAN

TIP

Have fun with your fungi! This soup is great with creminis, but I love it with other types of mushrooms too. Try swapping in shiitake, maitake, oyster, or enoki mushrooms, or use a mix of varieties.

Mushroom Farro Kale Soup

This recipe is my twist on mushroom barley soup, with chewy farro instead of barley and lots of kale. Tamari and rice vinegar might seem like unusual ingredients here, but trust me on this one! They really highlight the mushrooms' umami flavor, making the soup deeply savory. If you have leftover soup, freeze it for later. It reheats perfectly for a quick and easy lunch.

2 tablespoons extra-virgin olive oil

1 medium yellow onion, chopped

16 ounces cremini mushrooms, stemmed and sliced

½ teaspoon sea salt

½ teaspoon freshly ground black pepper

2 garlic cloves, grated

¼ cup dry white wine

4 cups vegetable broth

2 cups water

2½ tablespoons tamari

1 cup dry quick-cooking farro*

8 fresh thyme sprigs, bundled

1½ teaspoons rice vinegar

½ bunch kale, stemmed, leaves torn

Red pepper flakes (optional)

Heat the olive oil in a large pot over medium heat. Add the onion and cook, stirring occasionally, for 5 to 8 minutes, or until softened. Stir in the mushrooms, salt, and pepper and cook until tender, 8 to 10 minutes.

Stir in the garlic, then add the wine, broth, water, tamari, farro, and thyme bundle. Simmer, uncovered, for 25 minutes, or until the farro is tender. Remove the thyme bundle and stir in the rice vinegar. Add the kale and stir until wilted. Season to taste and serve with red pepper flakes, if desired.

*There are different types of farro. Seek out quick-cooking, or pearled, farro for this recipe because it requires the shortest time to cook.

SERVES 4

VEGAN

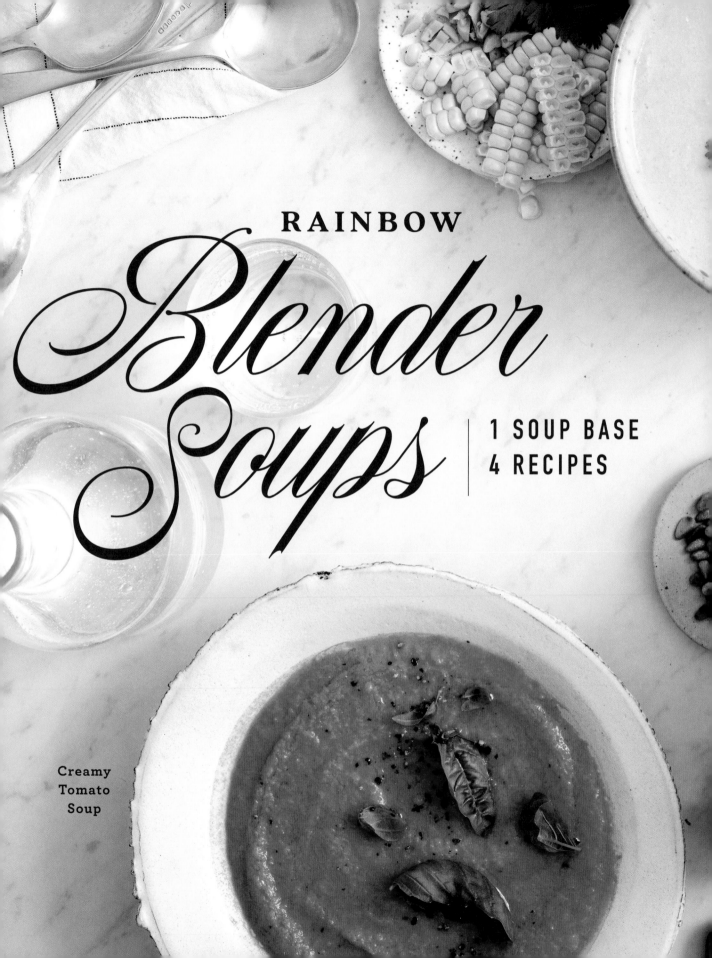

RAINBOW

Blender Soups

1 SOUP BASE
4 RECIPES

Creamy
Tomato
Soup

Lemongrass
Coconut Corn
Bisque

Beet Soup
with Cumin &
Crispy Chickpeas

Green
Chard Soup

Shared Soup Ingredients

2 tablespoons extra-virgin olive oil
1 medium yellow onion, chopped
2 garlic cloves, halved
½ teaspoon sea salt
Freshly ground black pepper

Heat the oil in a large pot over medium heat. Add the onion, garlic, salt, and several grinds of pepper and sauté for 5 to 8 minutes, or until softened. Follow individual recipe instructions for adding remaining ingredients.

SERVES 4

BEET SOUP WITH CUMIN & CRISPY CHICKPEAS

1½ pounds beets (3 to 4), peeled and diced
½ teaspoon ground coriander
½ teaspoon ground cumin
4 cups vegetable broth
¼ cup tahini
2 tablespoons fresh lemon juice
¼ teaspoon sea salt

To the onions, add the beets, coriander, and cumin and stir for 30 seconds. Add the broth and simmer for 20 minutes, or until the beets are tender. Transfer to a blender and add the tahini, lemon juice, and salt. Blend well and season to taste.

For garnish: Greek yogurt, chives, Roasted Chickpeas (page 72)

GREEN CHARD SOUP

4 cups cauliflower florets

3½ cups vegetable broth

1 bunch Swiss chard, stemmed, leaves torn

¼ cup fresh dill

1 tablespoon fresh lemon juice

¼ teaspoon Dijon mustard

¼ teaspoon sea salt

To the onions, add the cauliflower and broth and simmer for 20 minutes. Add the chard leaves during the last 5 minutes of cooking to wilt down. Transfer to a blender and add the dill, lemon juice, mustard, and salt. Blend well and season to taste.

For garnish: pine nuts, fresh dill

LEMONGRASS COCONUT CORN BISQUE

3 cups fresh corn kernels (from about 4 ears)

1 (14-ounce) can full-fat coconut milk

2¼ cups water

2 stalks lemongrass, outer leaves removed, cut into 4-inch pieces

½ teaspoon grated fresh ginger

2 tablespoons fresh lime juice

½ teaspoon sea salt

To the onions, add the corn, coconut milk, water, lemongrass, and ginger and simmer for 20 minutes. Remove and discard the lemongrass. Transfer to a blender and add the lime juice and salt. Blend well and season to taste.

For garnish: corn kernels, fresh cilantro, pinch of cayenne, toasted cashews or peanuts (page 78)

CREAMY TOMATO SOUP

1 medium carrot, chopped

1 (28-ounce) can diced tomatoes

½ cup cooked white beans, drained and rinsed

⅓ cup oil-packed sun-dried tomatoes

2½ cups vegetable broth

To the onions, add the carrots, diced tomatoes, beans, sun-dried tomatoes, and broth and simmer for 20 minutes. Transfer to a blender. Blend well and season to taste.

For garnish: fresh basil leaves, drizzles of extra-virgin olive oil

Farmers Market Vegetable Soup

When you come home with a beautiful bunch of carrots with lush tops, don't toss those tops . . . Make this soup! This recipe uses all parts of the carrot—you'll simmer the greens to create a flavorful broth and add the roots to the soup itself. Filled with fresh veggies, herbs, and nutty wild rice, this nourishing soup is perfect for early fall.

2 tablespoons extra-virgin olive oil, plus more for serving

½ medium yellow onion, chopped

1½ cups chopped carrots (3 to 4 medium)

2 celery stalks, chopped

½ teaspoon sea salt, plus more to taste

2 garlic cloves, grated

4 cups Carrot Top Broth* (page 99)

12 fresh thyme sprigs, bundled

1 cup chopped fresh green beans

1 small yellow squash or zucchini, chopped

1 cup cooked wild rice/brown rice blend (page 257)

1 tablespoon fresh lemon juice

¼ cup finely chopped fresh parsley

Crusty bread, for serving

Freshly ground black pepper

Heat the olive oil in a large pot over medium heat. Add the onion, carrots, celery, salt, and several grinds of pepper and cook, stirring occasionally, for 5 to 8 minutes, or until softened. Stir in the garlic, then add the broth and thyme bundle. Simmer, uncovered, for 20 minutes.

Add the green beans, squash, and rice and simmer for 8 minutes, or until the vegetables are tender.

Stir in the lemon juice and parsley. Season to taste and serve with drizzles of olive oil and crusty bread.

If using store-bought broth, increase the salt to ¾ teaspoon.

SERVES 4

GLUTEN-FREE | VEGAN

*This recipe is all about the broth! We don't recommend substituting store-bought here.

Tortellini Soup with Lemon Peel Broth

You may have noticed that there are quite a few lemons in the recipes in this book. Whenever a recipe calls for fresh lemon juice but not lemon zest, I peel the lemon before I juice it. I freeze the peels until I have enough to make this brightly flavored golden broth. Since the broth is so good on its own, I always pair it with simple ingredients, like the tortellini and fresh veggies here, to highlight its delicate flavor.

9 ounces store-bought tortellini

4 cups Lemon Peel Broth* (page 99)

2 cups fresh spinach

1 cup frozen peas, thawed

1 tablespoon fresh lemon juice

2 cups fresh basil leaves

Extra-virgin olive oil, for drizzling

Pinch of red pepper flakes (optional)

Sea salt and freshly ground black pepper

Bring a large pot of salted water to a boil. Prepare the tortellini according to the package instructions, cooking until al dente. Drain and set aside.

Warm the broth in a large pot or Dutch oven over medium-low heat until heated through, about 2 minutes. Add the cooked tortellini, spinach, peas, lemon juice, and half the basil. Stir until the spinach is wilted, about 1 minute. Season to taste.

Portion the soup into bowls and top with a drizzle of olive oil, the remaining basil, several grinds of pepper, and pinches of red pepper flakes, if desired.

SERVES 4

VEGAN: Use vegan tortellini (we like Kite Hill).

Brothy Potato Leek Soup

Whatever you do, don't ever toss the dark green tops of leeks. They're a magical addition to homemade vegetable stock, giving it sweet, oniony depth of flavor. I often have a stash of them in my freezer, ready and waiting to go into my next batch of broth. Now that you know that, I have a confession to make: we first developed this recipe using store-bought broth! We really liked it that way, and you could totally use store-bought broth in a pinch. But once we tried the leek broth here, we knew that it had to become part of the recipe. With it, this soup is ten times better.

2 tablespoons extra-virgin olive oil, plus more for drizzling

3½ cups chopped leeks, white and light green parts (about 3 leeks)

2 celery stalks, chopped

1 teaspoon sea salt

1½ teaspoons freshly ground black pepper

2 garlic cloves, grated

6 cups Leek Top Broth* (page 98)

12 ounces Yukon Gold potatoes, chopped

1½ cups chopped parsnips (1 to 2 parsnips)

⅓ cup dry green lentils, rinsed

1½ teaspoons herbes de Provence

1 tablespoon fresh lemon juice

Fresh parsley, for garnish

Heat the olive oil in a large pot over medium heat. Add the leeks, celery, salt, and pepper and cook, stirring occasionally, for 5 to 8 minutes, or until softened.

Stir in the garlic, then add the broth, potatoes, parsnips, lentils, and herbes de Provence. Simmer, uncovered, for 30 minutes. Stir in the lemon juice, drizzle with olive oil, and garnish with parsley. Season to taste and serve.

If using store-bought broth, add 8 fresh thyme sprigs, bundled, to the soup along with the broth. Remove before serving.

SERVES 4 TO 6

GLUTEN-FREE | VEGAN

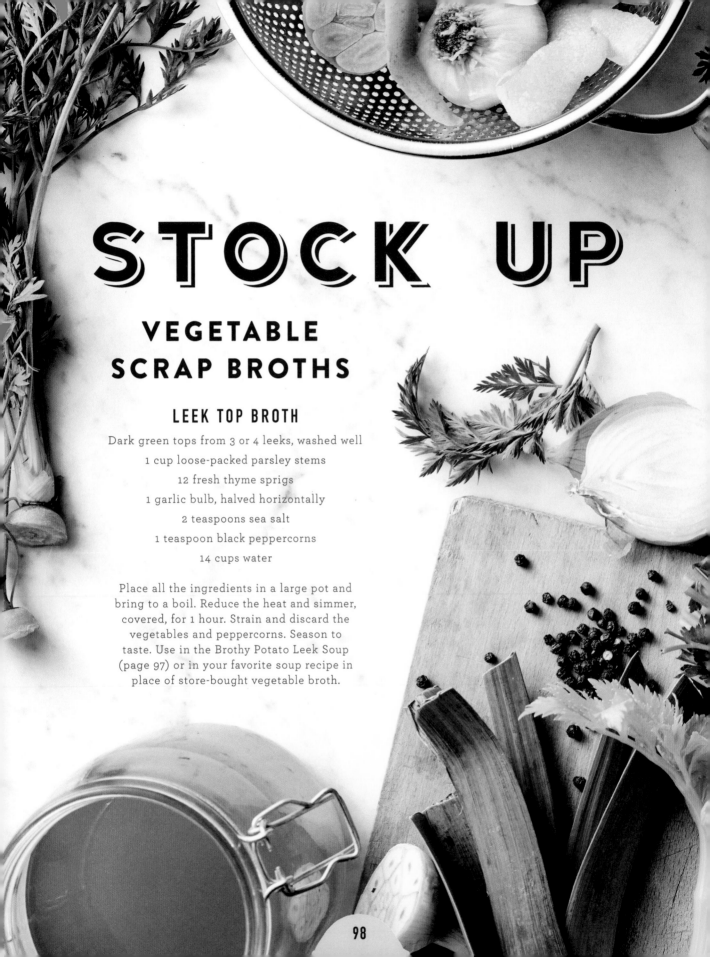

STOCK UP

VEGETABLE SCRAP BROTHS

LEEK TOP BROTH

Dark green tops from 3 or 4 leeks, washed well

1 cup loose-packed parsley stems

12 fresh thyme sprigs

1 garlic bulb, halved horizontally

2 teaspoons sea salt

1 teaspoon black peppercorns

14 cups water

Place all the ingredients in a large pot and bring to a boil. Reduce the heat and simmer, covered, for 1 hour. Strain and discard the vegetables and peppercorns. Season to taste. Use in the Brothy Potato Leek Soup (page 97) or in your favorite soup recipe in place of store-bought vegetable broth.

CARROT TOP BROTH

Tops from 1 bunch carrots, washed well

3 carrots, cut into big pieces

½ yellow onion

1 garlic bulb, halved horizontally

Stems from 1 bunch fresh parsley

2 teaspoons sea salt

1 teaspoon black peppercorns

12 cups water

Place all the ingredients in a large pot and bring to a boil. Reduce the heat and simmer, covered, for 1 hour. Strain and discard the vegetables and peppercorns. Season to taste. Use in the Farmers Market Vegetable Soup (page 93) or in your favorite soup recipe in place of store-bought vegetable broth.

TO STORE BROTH:

Allow it to cool to room temperature after cooking. Transfer it to airtight containers and refrigerate for up to 1 week or freeze for up to 3 months.

LEMON PEEL BROTH

4 celery stalks, including leaves

2 garlic bulbs, halved horizontally

Peels from 4 lemons

2 teaspoons sea salt

1 teaspoon black peppercorns

10 cups water

Place all the ingredients in a large pot and bring to a boil. Reduce the heat and simmer, covered, for 30 minutes. Strain and discard the vegetables, peppercorns, and lemon peels. Season to taste. Use in the Tortellini Soup with Lemon Peel Broth (page 95) or in your favorite soup recipe in place of store-bought vegetable broth.

CHAPTER
— 4 —
DINNER

DINNER

3-IN-1 PANTRY-POWERED MEAL PLANS

TIP

No grill? No problem. Make this recipe in the oven instead! Roast the chickpeas at 425°F for 20 to 30 minutes, or until golden brown and crisp. Roast the broccoli, cut side down, for 15 to 20 minutes, or until it's browned underneath. Flip and roast for another 5 minutes, or until the florets are crisp and the stem is tender.

Broccoli Steaks with Chickpea Romesco

If you've never tried grilled broccoli before, get ready—you're in for a treat! The stem becomes perfectly tender, and the florets get nicely charred. I love to serve it with tangy romesco sauce to accent its smoky flavor. Romesco, a Spanish tomato and pepper sauce, is traditionally thickened with nuts and bread. In this version, I use chickpeas instead, which make the sauce really smooth and creamy.

COUSCOUS

1 cup water

1 cup dry couscous

1 tablespoon plus 1 teaspoon extra-virgin olive oil

½ teaspoon sea salt

¼ cup chopped fresh parsley

1½ teaspoons fresh lemon juice

FOR THE BROCCOLI

4 small to medium heads broccoli with stems

Extra-virgin olive oil, for drizzling

¾ cup cooked chickpeas, drained and rinsed (page 72)

Chickpea Romesco (page 76)

¼ cup chopped almonds

Lemon zest, for garnish

Sea salt and freshly ground black pepper

Make the couscous: Bring the water to a boil in a medium saucepan. Add the couscous, 1 teaspoon of the olive oil, and the salt and stir. Cover, remove from the heat, and let sit for 10 minutes, or until the couscous is tender and all the liquid has been absorbed. When ready to serve, fluff with a fork and toss with the parsley, lemon juice, and the remaining 1 tablespoon olive oil.

Preheat a grill or grill pan to medium-high heat.

Prepare the broccoli: Cut the broccoli in half lengthwise and trim off the long part of the stem, leaving enough of it to keep the "steak" intact. Drizzle generously with olive oil and season generously with salt and pepper. Use your hands to coat both sides. Place the chickpeas on a big piece of foil in a single layer. Drizzle with olive oil, season with salt and pepper, and toss to coat.

Grill the broccoli, cut side down, for 10 minutes, with a piece of foil loosely covering it. Flip and cook for 4 to 7 more minutes, or until both sides are well charred and tender. Place the foil with the chickpeas on the grill and cook for 8 to 10 minutes, or until charred on one side. Toss and cook for 2 more minutes.

Assemble plates with a swoosh of the romesco sauce, the couscous, and two broccoli steaks each. Top with the chickpeas and almonds and garnish with lemon zest.

SERVES 4

GLUTEN-FREE: Replace the couscous with cooked quinoa (page 71).

VEGAN

Top these enchiladas with fresh garnishes like cilantro, diced white onion, radishes, and thinly sliced jalapeño or serrano peppers for a pop of color and crunch!

Creamy Cauliflower Enchiladas

Cauliflower is one versatile veggie, and these enchiladas are here to prove it! You'll use it in two ways, rolling some roasted cauliflower into the enchilada filling and blending more into the zesty, creamy sauce. Top the enchiladas with cheese for extra richness (and a crave-worthy cheese pull!), or skip it for a lighter vegan version. We love them both ways!

1 small head cauliflower

8 ounces cremini mushrooms, quartered

½ medium white onion, cut into wedges

1 jalapeño pepper, stemmed and halved

1 unpeeled garlic clove

1 cup water

⅓ cup raw cashews

¼ cup extra-virgin olive oil, plus more for drizzling

2 tablespoons fresh lime juice, plus wedges for serving

1 teaspoon ground coriander

1 teaspoon ground cumin

1 teaspoon sea salt, plus more for sprinkling

½ cup fresh cilantro

8 tortillas, warmed (I like a corn and flour blend)

¾ cup grated Monterey Jack cheese (optional)

Desired toppings

Freshly ground black pepper

Preheat the oven to 425°F. Line two baking sheets with parchment paper and brush a 9×13-inch baking dish with olive oil.

Chop the cauliflower florets and cores into small pieces and place on one of the baking sheets. Place the mushrooms, onion, jalapeño, and garlic clove on the second baking sheet. Drizzle with olive oil and sprinkle with salt and pepper and roast for 20 to 25 minutes, or until the vegetables are golden brown and tender. When cool to the touch, chop the onions.

Measure 1½ cups of the roasted cauliflower and place in a blender with half of the roasted onions, the jalapeño, peeled roasted garlic, water, cashews, olive oil, lime juice, coriander, cumin, salt, and several grinds of pepper. Blend until creamy. Add the cilantro and pulse to combine.

Spread ½ cup of the sauce at the bottom of the prepared baking dish. Fill each tortilla with a spoonful of the remaining sauce, the mushrooms, and the remaining cauliflower and onions. Roll and place each tortilla in the baking dish seam side down. Top with the remaining sauce and sprinkle with the cheese, if using. Bake, covered, for 20 minutes. If using the cheese, uncover and broil for 3 to 5 minutes, or until the cheese is browned and bubbling.

Remove from the oven and top with desired toppings. Serve with lime wedges.

SERVES 4 | **GLUTEN-FREE:** Use gluten-free tortillas. | **VEGAN:** Skip the cheese.

Spring Pea Fritters with Whipped Feta

If you have frozen peas and eggs on hand, you're halfway to making these easy one-bowl fritters! The peas, lemon zest, and dill fill them with bright, fresh flavor, making this one of my favorite light meals in the spring. Serve with dollops of tangy whipped feta and a simple green salad tossed with the lemon vinaigrette on page 135.

WHIPPED FETA

4 ounces feta cheese, crumbled (1 cup)

2½ tablespoons extra-virgin olive oil

1½ tablespoons fresh lemon juice

1½ teaspoons water

FRITTERS

3 large eggs

3 cups frozen peas, thawed and patted dry

1½ cups chopped scallions (about 1 bunch)

⅓ cup finely chopped fresh dill,
plus more for garnish

3 garlic cloves, grated

1 tablespoon lemon zest

¾ teaspoon sea salt

1½ cups panko bread crumbs

3 tablespoons all-purpose flour

Avocado oil, for the pan

Freshly ground black pepper

Make the whipped feta: In a small food processor, place the feta, olive oil, lemon juice, and water and pulse until creamy.

Make the fritters: In a large bowl, whisk the eggs. Add the peas, scallions, dill, garlic, lemon zest, salt, and several grinds of pepper. Use a potato masher to mash the mixture, keeping a decent amount of pea pieces intact. Add the panko, sprinkle in the flour, and fold to combine.

Heat a cast-iron skillet over medium heat. Use a ¼-cup measuring cup to form the pea mixture into 14 to 16 patties. The mixture might seem loose at this point, but the patties will firm up as they cook. Coat the skillet generously with oil. Cook the patties for 3 to 4 minutes on the first side, flip, and cook for 2 to 3 more minutes, or until firm and lightly browned, working in batches as necessary.

Garnish with fresh dill and serve with the whipped feta.

SERVES 4

Baked Tomato Fennel Risotto

A classic stovetop risotto has its time and place. Jack and I love making one for at-home date nights, when we don't mind standing at the stove for thirty-plus minutes, stirring the entire time. But when I'm entertaining or cooking on a busy weeknight, all that stirring doesn't sound so fun. That's where this oven risotto comes in. It has a slightly longer cooking time than most of the At the Ready recipes in this book, but it's super hands-off. The first time I served it to my extended family, my mom exclaimed, "I didn't see you make risotto!" You can effortlessly bring it from the oven to the table, (almost) no stirring required.

2 tablespoons extra-virgin olive oil

2 shallots, diced (⅔ cup)

2 medium fennel bulbs, chopped

1½ cups dry Arborio rice

½ cup dry white wine

2 pints cherry tomatoes

2 garlic cloves, grated

¾ cup grated pecorino cheese, plus more for serving

1 teaspoon sea salt

4 cups vegetable broth

½ cup fresh basil leaves

¼ cup pine nuts

Freshly ground black pepper

Preheat the oven to 400°F.

Heat the olive oil in a large Dutch oven over medium heat. Add the shallots and fennel and cook, stirring occasionally, for 5 minutes, or until softened. Add the rice and cook, stirring, for 2 minutes. Stir in the wine and let it cook down for 30 seconds, then stir in half the tomatoes, the garlic, cheese, salt, and several grinds of pepper. Stir in the broth. Cover and bake for 30 minutes.

Remove the pot from the oven and stir the rice. Add the remaining tomatoes on top. Cover and bake for an additional 10 minutes. Remove from the oven and stir again. It should still be a bit liquidy at this point, but it will thicken as it sits. Let sit, covered, for 15 minutes. Stir in half the basil. Garnish with the remaining basil and half the pine nuts.

Serve with the remaining pine nuts and more grated cheese, if desired.

SERVES 6 TO 8

GLUTEN-FREE

Shredded Brussels Sprouts White Pizza

My whole family loves this pizza. When I first made it, I served it alongside a regular cheese pizza, thinking I would be the only one to like this vegan combination. To my surprise, everyone asked, "What is that sauce?!" and went back for seconds. The entire pizza disappeared in minutes!

1 pound pizza dough, store-bought or homemade (page 258)

Extra-virgin olive oil, for brushing

Basic Cashew Cream (page 256)

1½ cups thinly sliced Brussels sprouts (3 ounces)

½ cup thinly sliced red onion

Red pepper flakes

⅓ cup fresh basil leaves, torn if large

Preheat the oven to 500°F.

Stretch the dough on a 14-inch pizza pan and brush the edges of the crust with olive oil. Place a heaping ⅓ cup of the cashew cream in the center of the dough and spread into a thin layer. Sprinkle with the Brussels sprouts, red onion, and pinches of red pepper flakes. Bake for 11 to 15 minutes, or until the crust is browned and cooked through.

Stir water into the remaining cashew cream, 1 tablespoon at a time, to reach a drizzleable consistency. Remove the pizza from the oven, drizzle generously with the cashew cream, top with the basil, and serve.

SERVES 2 TO 3

VEGAN

Creamy Orzo with Asparagus & Peas

This quick orzo pasta is a great back-pocket weeknight recipe. It has the same luxurious texture and rich flavor as risotto, but it cooks in a fraction of the time! I love how this fresh medley of spring veggies contrasts with the creamy base, but feel free to switch the vegetables based on the season. Grilled or sautéed zucchini, blanched broccolini, or sautéed broccoli rabe would be lovely here too.

¼ cup extra-virgin olive oil

2 leeks, white and light green parts, chopped (3 cups)

1 teaspoon sea salt

½ cup dry white wine

2 garlic cloves, grated

12 ounces orzo pasta

3½ to 4 cups vegetable broth

2 teaspoons lemon zest, plus more for garnish

1 bunch asparagus, trimmed and chopped into 1-inch pieces

¾ cup frozen peas

2 teaspoons fresh lemon juice, plus wedges for serving

Fresh herbs (basil and/or tarragon), for garnish

Microgreens, for garnish (optional)

Freshly ground black pepper

Heat 3 tablespoons of the olive oil in a medium Dutch oven over medium heat. Add the leeks, ¾ teaspoon of the salt, and several grinds of pepper and cook for 5 minutes, or until softened. Stir in the wine and let it cook down for 30 seconds. Reduce the heat to low and add the garlic, orzo, and 3 cups of the broth. Stir, cover, and let cook for 10 minutes, stirring occasionally to prevent sticking. Uncover and stir in the lemon zest and another ½ cup of the broth. Cook, stirring, over low heat for 2 to 4 minutes, or until the mixture is creamy and the orzo is cooked through.

Meanwhile, bring a medium pot of salted water to a boil. Drop the asparagus and peas into the boiling water and blanch for 1 to 2 minutes, or until tender but still bright green. Drain, transfer to a kitchen towel, and pat dry. Transfer the vegetables to a large bowl and toss with the remaining 1 tablespoon olive oil, the remaining ¼ teaspoon salt, the lemon juice, and several grinds of pepper.

Before serving, check the orzo's consistency. If it has thickened too much, stir in the remaining ½ cup broth. Portion the orzo into bowls and top with the vegetable mixture. Garnish with fresh herbs, lemon zest, and microgreens, if using. Season to taste and serve with lemon wedges.

SERVES 4

VEGAN

MAKE THIS RECIPE VEGAN!

In a medium bowl, combine 1½ cups cooked white beans, 2 tablespoons olive oil, 1 tablespoon fresh lemon juice, 1 teaspoon sea salt, and several grinds of pepper. Use a potato masher to mash until the mixture is creamy and spreadable with a few bean pieces still visible. Use in the sandwiches in place of the mozzarella.

Grilled Zucchini Sandwiches

A great sandwich starts with a great condiment, and I'm obsessed with the red pepper tapenade in this one. It's tangy and briny like traditional tapenade, but it has a little sweetness from the roasted red pepper and basil. I love pairing it with grilled zucchini and creamy fresh mozzarella, but for an equally delicious vegan sandwich, you can sub lemony smashed white beans for the cheese.

RED PEPPER TAPENADE

1 cup jarred roasted red peppers

½ cup pitted kalamata olives

⅓ cup fresh basil leaves

1 tablespoon capers

1 tablespoon extra-virgin olive oil

1½ teaspoons fresh lemon juice

1 teaspoon honey or maple syrup

1 small garlic clove, grated

Sea salt and freshly ground black pepper

FOR THE SANDWICHES

2 medium zucchini

Extra-virgin olive oil, for drizzling

8 slices sourdough or country bread

8 ounces fresh mozzarella

Fresh basil leaves

Sea salt and freshly ground black pepper

Make the red pepper tapenade: In a small food processor, place the red peppers, olives, basil, capers, olive oil, lemon juice, honey, and garlic. Pulse until just combined, so that the tapenade is still chunky. Season to taste with salt and pepper and chill until ready to use.

Make the sandwiches: Preheat a grill or grill pan to medium heat. Slice the zucchini lengthwise into ¼-inch planks, drizzle with olive oil, and season with salt and pepper. Grill for 2 minutes per side, or until char marks form and the zucchini is tender but still has some bite. Assemble each sandwich on the bread with the tapenade, zucchini, mozzarella, and basil.

SERVES 4

GLUTEN-FREE: Use gluten-free bread.

Chickpea Cacio e Pepe

This recipe is my vegan spin on the classic Roman dish cacio e pepe, which simply translates to "cheese and pepper." Instead of using cheese to create the creamy sauce, I blend chickpeas with starchy pasta water and miso paste, which adds the savory, umami flavor that would typically come from the pecorino. Since this pasta is so simple, I like to serve it with a fresh veggie side dish like sautéed kale dressed with a squeeze of lemon.

12 ounces bucatini, spaghetti, or linguine pasta

¾ cup cooked chickpeas, drained and rinsed (page 72)

¼ cup extra-virgin olive oil

3 tablespoons white miso paste

2 tablespoons nutritional yeast

1 teaspoon freshly ground black pepper

½ to 1 cup reserved pasta water

Vegan Parmesan Cheese (page 259), for serving (optional)

Lemon wedges, for serving (optional)

Sea salt

Bring a large pot of salted water to a boil. Prepare the pasta according to the package instructions, cooking until al dente. During the last few minutes of cooking, scoop out 1 cup of the hot pasta water.

In a blender, place the chickpeas, olive oil, miso paste, nutritional yeast, ½ teaspoon of the black pepper, and ½ cup of the reserved pasta water and blend until creamy.

Drain the pasta and return it to the pot. Stir in the sauce. It should be lightly creamy. If it's too thick, add up to ½ cup more pasta water.

Serve with the remaining ½ teaspoon black pepper and vegan Parmesan and lemon wedges, if desired.

SERVES 4　　　**GLUTEN-FREE:** Use gluten-free pasta.　　**VEGAN**

Savory Vegetable Cabbage Pancakes

I always seem to have part of a cabbage and a few carrots in the back of my fridge, so these savory pancakes are a favorite go-to dinner. Enjoy them on their own, or serve them with cooked rice (page 71) for a larger meal. If you have any pancakes left over, they're great for breakfast the next morning.

1½ cups all-purpose flour, spooned and leveled (see page 23)

2¼ teaspoons baking powder

1½ teaspoons sea salt

¾ teaspoon cane sugar

3 large eggs

¾ cup water

1½ teaspoons avocado oil, plus more for the pan

3 cups shredded green cabbage

1½ bunches scallions, sliced into thin strips, plus more for garnish

3 medium carrots, julienned (1½ cups)

TAMARI DIPPING SAUCE

3 tablespoons water

2 tablespoons cane sugar

2 tablespoons rice vinegar

2 tablespoons tamari

1 tablespoon fresh lime juice

SPICY MAYO DIPPING SAUCE

¼ cup mayonnaise

1 tablespoon sriracha

In a large bowl, whisk together the flour, baking powder, salt, and sugar.

In a medium bowl, whisk together the eggs, water, and avocado oil. Pour the wet ingredients into the dry ingredients and mix until just combined. Fold in the cabbage, scallions, and carrots and set aside for 10 minutes.

Make the dipping sauces: In a small bowl, mix together the water, sugar, rice vinegar, tamari, and lime juice. In another small bowl, stir together the mayonnaise and sriracha.

Heat a large nonstick skillet over low heat and brush with oil. Use a ¼-cup measuring cup to scoop the batter into the skillet. Cook for 3 to 4 minutes per side, or until golden brown and cooked through. Repeat with the remaining batter, wiping out the skillet and brushing with more oil as needed.

Garnish with scallions and serve with the tamari and spicy mayo dipping sauces.

SERVES 4

Nourish Bowls with Miso Citrus Dressing

These are the ultimate feel-good bowls! They're so wholesome, light, and fresh—yet super flavorful too. The earthy steamed veggies contrast beautifully with the zippy orange and miso dressing, and a little sauerkraut adds the perfect funky pop. If you can't find adzuki beans, use black beans (page 72) or roasted chickpeas (page 72) instead.

1 pound daikon radishes, cut into thin wedges or half-moons

1 watermelon radish, cut into thin wedges or half-moons

1 sweet potato, cut into thin wedges or half-moons

1 bunch lacinato kale, stemmed, leaves torn

Miso Citrus Dressing (page 77)

2 cups cooked brown rice (page 71)

1½ cups cooked adzuki beans, drained and rinsed (page 72)

½ cup sauerkraut

Sesame seeds, for sprinkling

Microgreens, for garnish

Place the radishes and sweet potato in a steamer basket and set over a large pot filled with 1 inch of water. Bring the water to a simmer, cover, and steam for 8 to 10 minutes, or until the vegetables are tender.

Meanwhile, in a large bowl, massage the kale with a bit of the dressing until the leaves are soft and wilted.

Assemble the bowls with the brown rice, beans, radishes, sweet potato, kale, and sauerkraut. Drizzle each bowl with some of the dressing and sprinkle with sesame seeds. Garnish with microgreens and serve with the remaining dressing on the side.

SERVES 4 | **GLUTEN-FREE:** Use certified gluten-free tamari in the dressing. | **VEGAN**

Cozy Autumn Pasta Bake

To me, "feel-good food" means two different things, depending on the season.
In the summer, it refers to food that's fresh and bright. But in the winter,
it's all about comfort. On a freezing-cold night, nothing feels better than
digging in to this cheesy baked pasta. Filled with hearty roasted vegetables
and topped with crispy bread crumbs, it's comfort food at its finest.

4 cups thinly sliced Brussels sprouts
(6 ounces)

1 cup peeled and finely diced butternut
squash

⅓ cup thinly sliced red onion

10 ounces fusilli pasta

2 tablespoons chopped fresh sage leaves

1 tablespoon balsamic vinegar

1 tablespoon extra-virgin olive oil,
plus more for drizzling

2 garlic cloves, grated

¾ teaspoon sea salt, plus more for sprinkling

1 cup whole milk ricotta cheese

1 cup grated Gruyère cheese

2 tablespoons grated pecorino cheese

½ cup coarsely ground fresh bread crumbs
(page 257)

Fresh parsley leaves, for garnish (optional)

Freshly ground black pepper

Preheat the oven to 425°F. Line a baking
sheet with parchment paper and brush an
8×8-inch baking dish with olive oil.

Place the Brussels sprouts, squash, and onion
on the baking sheet. Drizzle with olive oil,
sprinkle with salt and pepper, and toss to
coat. Spread evenly on the baking sheet and
roast for 10 to 13 minutes, or until the squash
is tender and the Brussels sprouts are just
beginning to brown.

Meanwhile, bring a large pot of salted water
to a boil. Prepare the pasta according to the
package instructions, cooking until al dente.
Drain.

In a large bowl, combine the roasted veggies,
cooked pasta, sage, balsamic vinegar, olive
oil, garlic, salt, and several grinds of pepper.
Transfer half the mixture to the prepared
baking dish and evenly dollop the ricotta on top.

Add the remaining pasta mixture and top
with the Gruyère, pecorino, and bread
crumbs. Drizzle with olive oil, cover, and
bake for 8 minutes. Uncover and bake for
10 to 12 minutes, or until the top is browned
and bubbling. Garnish with fresh parsley, if
using, and serve.

SERVES 4

Savory Oats with Crispy Mushrooms

Who says oats are just for breakfast? Or that they have to be sweet?
Here, I top creamy steel-cut oats with savory garnishes like roasted
shiitake mushrooms, crisp veggies, and soft-boiled eggs to create a
simple, fresh, and filling dinner. To make this recipe even quicker to
prepare, top the bowls with avocado slices instead of eggs.

4 ounces shiitake mushrooms, stemmed and thinly sliced

1 tablespoon extra-virgin olive oil

1½ teaspoons tamari, plus more for serving

3 cups water

1 cup steel-cut oats

¼ teaspoon sea salt

Rice vinegar, for drizzling

4 soft-boiled eggs (page 73)

2 small red radishes, thinly sliced

2 tablespoons sliced scallions

2 tablespoons pickled ginger

Sesame seeds, for sprinkling

Nori or toasted seaweed snacks, sliced

Preheat the oven to 350°F and line a baking sheet with parchment paper.

Place the mushrooms on the baking sheet and toss with the olive oil and tamari until well coated. Spread evenly on the baking sheet and bake for 20 to 30 minutes, or until the mushrooms are shriveled up and lightly crisp, tossing halfway through.

Meanwhile, bring the water to a boil in a medium pot. Add the oats and salt and reduce the heat to medium-low. Cook, stirring occasionally, for 15 to 20 minutes, or until thickened.

Portion the oats into bowls and top with the mushrooms, a drizzle of rice vinegar, the eggs, radishes, scallions, pickled ginger, sesame seeds, and nori. Serve with tamari on the side.

SERVES 4

GLUTEN-FREE: Use certified gluten-free oats and tamari.

VEGAN: Skip the eggs and add avocado slices.

This recipe would be a great vegan main at Thanksgiving or at any autumn meal!

Sage & Nut Stuffed Delicata Squash

When delicata squash appears at the farmers market each fall, I can hardly wait to bring it home and cook it. It has a sweet, concentrated flavor and skin so tender that there's no need to peel it. In this recipe, I fill the roasted squash with a creamy sage and cashew filling and sprinkle it with a crisp, nutty pecan topping. It's hearty, satisfying, and packed with fall flavor.

FOR THE SQUASH

3 medium delicata squash

Extra-virgin olive oil, for drizzling

Sea salt and freshly ground black pepper

TOPPING

⅓ cup whole rolled oats

¼ cup pecans

¼ cup walnuts

2 teaspoons maple syrup

½ teaspoon sea salt

Fresh parsley or sage leaves, for garnish

Freshly ground black pepper

FILLING

1¾ cups raw cashews

1½ tablespoons apple cider vinegar

1 tablespoon nutritional yeast

1 garlic clove

Pinch of nutmeg

½ teaspoon sea salt

½ cup water

5 fresh sage leaves

Freshly ground black pepper

Preheat the oven to 425°F and line a baking sheet with parchment paper.

Roast the squash: Slice the squash in half lengthwise and scoop out the seeds. Drizzle the inside of each half with olive oil and season very generously with salt and pepper. Roast cut side down for 20 to 25 minutes, or until tender and golden brown around the edges.

Make the topping: In a food processor, place the oats, pecans, walnuts, maple syrup, salt, and several grinds of pepper and pulse until just combined. Transfer to a bowl and set aside.

Make the filling: In the food processor (no need to wash it), place the cashews, vinegar, nutritional yeast, garlic, nutmeg, salt, and several grinds of pepper. Process until very finely ground, then add the water and process until smooth. Add the sage leaves and pulse until just incorporated.

Spoon the filling into the roasted squash halves, top with the crumble, and bake for 5 to 10 minutes, or until the topping is toasted. Garnish with parsley and serve.

SERVES 4 TO 6 | **GLUTEN-FREE:** Use certified gluten-free oats. | **VEGAN**

MIX & MATCH | VEGGIE

TACOS

CHOOSE A VEGETABLE FILLING:

CARROTS	**BUTTERNUT SQUASH**	**MIXED MUSHROOMS**	**CORN & ZUCCHINI**
1 pound	4 cups	20 ounces	kernels from 3 ears
cut into big chunks	peeled and cubed	stemmed and sliced	and 2 zucchini, diced

Toss with drizzles of avocado oil, ½ teaspoon ground coriander, ½ teaspoon ground cumin, ½ teaspoon salt, and pepper. For the mushrooms, skip the salt and add 1½ tablespoons tamari. Spread in a single layer on one or two baking sheets, as needed. Roast at 425°F for 20 to 30 minutes, or until tender and browned. Season to taste.

CHOOSE A SAUCE:

AVOCADO CILANTRO LIME

1 cup fresh cilantro

1 avocado

2 tablespoons avocado oil

2 tablespoons fresh lime juice

1 small garlic clove

½ jalapeño pepper, chopped

½ teaspoon sea salt

Pulse in a food processor until smooth.

TOMATO MANGO SALSA FRESCA

1 mango, diced

1 Roma tomato, diced

1 jalapeño pepper, diced

¼ cup diced red onion

¼ cup chopped fresh cilantro

1 tablespoon fresh lime juice

½ teaspoon sea salt

Stir together in a medium bowl.

RANCH-Y YOGURT CREMA
(OR VEGAN RANCH, PAGE 77)

1 cup whole milk Greek yogurt

2 tablespoons mayonnaise

2 teaspoons fresh lime juice

½ teaspoon garlic powder

½ teaspoon onion powder

¼ teaspoon dried dill

¼ to ½ teaspoon sea salt

Stir together in a small bowl.

ASSEMBLE TACOS WITH:

8 warmed or grilled tortillas

A layer of refried beans or smashed avocado

Desired fixings: shredded cabbage, jalapeños, Cotija cheese, cilantro, toasted pepitas, or Pickled Onions (page 78)

Serve with lime wedges for squeezing.

SERVES 4

Sheet Pan Tempeh Fajitas

If you still need a reason to try tempeh, this is it. A simple maple-chipotle sauce infuses it with sweet and smoky flavor, making it a delicious, satisfying base for these sheet pan fajitas. You can easily make a quick guacamole and prep the other fixings while the tempeh and veggies roast. By the time the sheet pans come out of the oven, everything will be ready to eat!

FOR THE TEMPEH

8 ounces tempeh, cut into ¼-inch-thick strips

⅓ cup tomato paste

1½ tablespoons avocado oil

1½ tablespoons maple syrup

1½ teaspoons chipotle powder

Heaping ¼ teaspoon sea salt

FOR THE FAJITAS

1 green bell pepper, stemmed, seeded, and sliced into strips

1 red bell pepper, stemmed, seeded, and sliced into strips

½ red onion, sliced into thin wedges

Avocado oil, for drizzling

2 avocados

2 tablespoons fresh lime juice, plus wedges for serving

8 tortillas, warmed

Fresh cilantro

Cotija cheese (optional)

Hot sauce (optional)

Sea salt and freshly ground black pepper

Preheat the oven to 425°F and line two baking sheets with parchment paper.

Place the tempeh in a steamer basket and set over a pot filled with 1 inch of water. Bring the water to a simmer, cover, and steam for 10 minutes. Steaming helps the tempeh become more tender and able to soak up flavor.

In a medium bowl, whisk together the tomato paste, avocado oil, maple syrup, chipotle powder, and salt. Add the steamed tempeh and toss to coat. Transfer to one of the baking sheets. Place the peppers and onions on the second baking sheet. Drizzle with avocado oil and season with salt and pepper, toss to coat, and spread evenly on the baking sheet.

Roast the tempeh and the vegetables for 20 minutes. Remove the tempeh from the oven, turn on the broiler, and broil the peppers and onions for 2 to 5 minutes, or until lightly charred.

Make a quick guacamole by combining the avocados, lime juice, and ¼ teaspoon sea salt in a small bowl. Mash with the back of a fork.

Serve the tempeh and fajita veggies with the tortillas, guacamole, lime wedges, cilantro, cheese, and hot sauce, if desired.

SERVES 4 | **GLUTEN-FREE:** Use gluten-free tortillas. | **VEGAN:** Skip the cheese.

MAKE THIS RECIPE VEGAN!

Double the dressing and toss half with 2 cups cooked white beans. Assemble plates with the dressed beans in place of the feta. Serve with the remaining dressing on the side.

Spring Sheet Pan with Baked Feta

Every spring, I count down the days until the Chicago farmers markets open. One of the first vegetables to appear there is asparagus, and after a loooong winter, it's such a gift. This sheet pan dinner, with slabs of creamy feta and drizzles of lemon vinaigrette, is such a simple way to show off the delicate, crisp-tender spears.

1 pound new potatoes or Yukon Gold potatoes, cut into 1-inch pieces

1 pound asparagus, trimmed and cut into 2-inch pieces

1 (8-ounce) block feta cheese, cut into 4 planks

Extra-virgin olive oil, for drizzling

2 tablespoons chopped chives, for garnish

2 tablespoons chopped fresh dill, for garnish

Pea shoots, for garnish

4 chive blossoms, torn, for garnish (optional)

Sea salt and freshly ground black pepper

LEMON VINAIGRETTE

2 tablespoons extra-virgin olive oil

2 tablespoons fresh lemon juice

½ small garlic clove, grated

¼ teaspoon honey or maple syrup

Sea salt and freshly ground black pepper

Preheat the oven to 425°F and line two baking sheets with parchment paper.

Place the potatoes on one of the baking sheets and the asparagus and feta planks on the other. Drizzle everything with olive oil and season the vegetables with salt and pepper. Toss to coat and spread evenly on the baking sheets. Roast the potatoes for 30 minutes, or until golden brown. Roast the asparagus and feta for 10 to 14 minutes, or until the asparagus is crisp-tender.

Make the lemon vinaigrette: In a small lidded jar, combine the olive oil, lemon juice, garlic, honey, and a pinch of salt and pepper. Shake well.

Assemble plates with the roasted vegetables and a roasted feta plank. Drizzle with the dressing and garnish with the chives, dill, pea shoots, and chive blossoms, if using.

SERVES 4

GLUTEN-FREE

Eggplant Sheet Pan Shawarma

If you love big, bold flavors, you have to try this recipe! It's a veggie riff on Middle Eastern shawarma, with thinly sliced eggplant and sweet potatoes stepping in for the traditional meat. When the veggies come out of the oven, set them out on a big platter (or one of the sheet pans) with all the fixings, and let everyone assemble their own wraps.

SHAWARMA SPICE

1 tablespoon ground cumin

1 tablespoon smoked paprika

1½ teaspoons cinnamon

1½ teaspoons ground cardamom

1½ teaspoons ground turmeric

FOR THE VEGETABLES

1 medium eggplant, sliced into thin half-moons

1 sweet potato, sliced into thin half-moons

Extra-virgin olive oil, for drizzling

Sea salt and freshly ground black pepper

FOR SERVING

4 pitas, warmed

Tahini Yogurt (page 257)

2 Persian cucumbers, thinly sliced

Fresh mint, parsley, or cilantro sprigs

½ cup Pickled Onions (page 78, optional)

Aleppo pepper, for sprinkling (optional)

Lemon wedges

Preheat the oven to 450°F and line two large baking sheets with parchment paper.

Make the shawarma spice: In a small bowl, whisk together the cumin, smoked paprika, cinnamon, cardamom, and turmeric. Set aside 1 tablespoon and store the remaining spice for another use.

Roast the vegetables: Place the eggplant on one of the baking sheets and the sweet potatoes on the other. Generously drizzle the eggplant with olive oil, and lightly drizzle the sweet potatoes. Sprinkle 2 teaspoons of the shawarma spice over the eggplant and the remaining 1 teaspoon over the sweet potatoes. Season all the vegetables with salt and pepper. Toss to coat, spread evenly on the baking sheets, and roast for 25 to 30 minutes, or until the sweet potatoes are golden brown and the eggplant is tender, rotating the pans halfway through.

Assemble wraps in the pita with the tahini yogurt, roasted vegetables, cucumbers, mint, pickled onions, and sprinkles of Aleppo pepper, if desired. Serve with lemon wedges on the side.

SERVES 4 | **GLUTEN-FREE:** Use gluten-free pita. | **VEGAN:** Replace the tahini yogurt with homemade hummus (page 256).

Sheet Pan Tofu Kimchi Lettuce Wraps

I know what you're thinking: Can lettuce wraps be dinner? In this case, absolutely! These fresh wraps are more substantial than they might seem, filled with meaty roasted mushrooms, tofu, rice, and a rich and creamy sauce made with spicy Korean gochujang. If you're new to cooking with gochujang, you can find it in Asian supermarkets or in many well-stocked grocery stores. Made with chiles, glutinous rice, fermented soybeans, salt, and sugar, it's spicy, funky, and absolutely delicious. A jar lasts for months in the fridge. I love keeping it on hand to season soups, veggies, and sauces like the one here.

2 portobello mushrooms, stemmed and sliced

7 ounces shiitake mushrooms, stemmed and halved

14 ounces extra-firm tofu, patted dry and cubed

¼ cup tamari

2 tablespoons avocado oil

FOR SERVING

12 butter lettuce leaves

2 cups cooked rice (page 71)

½ cup kimchi, chopped

3 scallions, chopped

2 Persian cucumbers, julienned

1 large carrot, julienned

Cashew Gochujang Sauce (page 76)

Preheat the oven to 425°F and line two baking sheets with parchment paper.

Place the mushrooms on one of the baking sheets and the tofu on the other. Toss the mushrooms and tofu with the tamari and avocado oil and spread evenly on the baking sheets. Roast for 30 minutes, or until the mushrooms and tofu are browned and crisp around the edges, rotating the pans halfway through.

Assemble the wraps with the lettuce leaves, roasted mushrooms and tofu, rice, kimchi, scallions, cucumbers, carrots, and drizzles of cashew gochujang sauce.

SERVES 4 | **GLUTEN-FREE:** Use certified gluten-free tamari. | **VEGAN:** Use vegan kimchi.

White Bean Swiss Chard Burgers

I rarely make veggie burgers in an attempt to replicate meat. Instead, I like to highlight a vegetable! These beans-and-greens burgers use Swiss chard in two ways. You'll incorporate the greens into the patties and quick-pickle the stems to create a tangy, crunchy, and colorful topping. The burgers turn out best if you chill them overnight in the fridge before you cook them. Feel free to make the pickled chard stems and the yogurt sauce in advance as well.

1 bunch Swiss chard, stems removed and set aside

3 cups cooked butter beans, drained and rinsed (page 72)

½ medium yellow onion, grated on the large holes of a box grater (⅓ cup)

3 garlic cloves, grated

3 tablespoons mayonnaise

1 tablespoon Dijon mustard

1 tablespoon chopped fresh dill or 1 teaspoon dried

1 teaspoon lemon zest

1 teaspoon sea salt

1 teaspoon freshly ground black pepper

¼ teaspoon cayenne pepper

1 large egg

1 cup panko bread crumbs

Avocado oil, for the pan

6 hamburger buns

Desired fixings: sunflower sprouts, lettuce, avocado, sliced cucumbers, etc.

PICKLED CHARD STEMS

Stems from 1 bunch Swiss chard, chopped (1¼ cups)

½ cup diced red onion

2 tablespoons fresh lemon juice

½ teaspoon sea salt

LEMON DILL YOGURT

½ cup whole milk Greek yogurt

1 teaspoon fresh lemon juice

1 teaspoon chopped fresh dill or ¼ teaspoon dried

¼ teaspoon sea salt

recipe continues

Roughly chop the chard leaves, place in a steamer basket, and set over a pot filled with 1 inch of water. Bring the water to a simmer, cover, and steam for 1 minute, or until the leaves are wilted. When cool to the touch, squeeze the excess water out of the leaves and chop finely.

In a large bowl, combine the chard with the beans, onion, garlic, mayonnaise, mustard, dill, lemon zest, salt, pepper, and cayenne. Use a potato masher to mash until the mixture holds together but still has some visible bean chunks. Add the egg and fold until combined. Then, fold in the panko. The mixture should be cohesive and a little wet.

Form the mixture into 6 patties. Place the patties on a baking sheet, cover loosely with foil or plastic wrap, and chill overnight.

Make the pickled chard stems: In a lidded jar, combine the chard stems, onion, lemon juice, and salt. Shake to combine and chill until ready to use.

Make the lemon dill yogurt: In a small bowl, combine the yogurt, lemon juice, dill, and salt. Chill until ready to use.

Preheat the oven to 400°F and line a baking sheet with parchment paper.

Heat a cast-iron skillet over medium heat. Coat the bottom with oil and cook the burgers for 3 to 4 minutes per side, or until browned, working in batches and reducing the heat to low as needed. Transfer the burgers to the prepared baking sheet and bake for 15 minutes. If desired, warm the buns in the oven during the last few minutes of cook time.

Assemble the burgers on the buns with the yogurt sauce, pickled chard stems, and desired fixings.

SERVES 6

Got leftover burgers? They freeze perfectly!
To thaw cooked and frozen patties, bake them in a 400°F
oven for 10 to 20 minutes, or until heated through.

Butternut & Thyme Galette

This galette is exactly what I want to make after a visit to the farmers market in the fall, when squash has just come into season. It's a bit of a project, so I often make two—one for now and one to freeze and bake later. It comes out delicious both ways, and as it bakes, the squash, onions, and buttery pastry will make your kitchen smell amazing.

FOR THE DOUGH

1 cup all-purpose flour, spooned and leveled (see page 23)

1 cup almond flour, spooned and leveled (see page 23)

½ teaspoon sea salt

6 tablespoons cold unsalted butter, cubed

¼ cup ice water

FOR THE FILLING

Neck of 1 small butternut squash, peeled and thinly sliced into half-moons (9 ounces)

1 cup thinly sliced red onion

1 tablespoon extra-virgin olive oil

1 teaspoon balsamic vinegar

½ teaspoon sea salt

1 tablespoon fresh thyme leaves, plus more for garnish

3 tablespoons crumbled feta cheese

1 large egg, beaten

Sesame seeds, for sprinkling

Freshly ground black pepper

Make the dough: In a food processor, place the all-purpose flour, almond flour, and salt and pulse to combine. Add the butter and pulse until crumbly. Add the ice water and pulse until the dough comes together. It should still be crumbly but hold together when pinched, and tiny specks of butter should be visible throughout it. Turn the dough out onto a piece of parchment paper and form into a ball. Flatten into a 1½-inch-thick disk, wrap in plastic wrap, and chill for at least 1 hour and up to 2 days.

Make the filling: Place the squash and half the onions in a large bowl and toss with the oil, vinegar, salt, and several grinds of pepper.

If baking right away, preheat the oven to 400°F.

Place the dough between two sheets of parchment paper and roll into a 12-inch circle. Remove the top sheet and transfer the dough and the bottom sheet to a large

recipe continues

145

baking sheet. Sprinkle the thyme around the center of the dough, followed by the remaining onions and 2 tablespoons of the feta. Layer on the butternut squash mixture and the remaining 1 tablespoon feta, leaving a 1½-inch border all around. Garnish with more thyme and fold the edges of the dough toward the squash, leaving the center of the filling exposed.

To bake: Brush the crust with the beaten egg and sprinkle with sesame seeds. Loosely cover with foil and bake for 1 hour to 1 hour and 15 minutes, or until the squash is tender when pierced with a paring knife. Remove the foil and bake for another 10 to 15 minutes, or until the crust is golden brown. Slice and serve.

Make-ahead option 1—One day in advance: Assemble the galette, but wait to brush with the beaten egg and sprinkle with sesame seeds. Cover with foil and refrigerate overnight. The next day, brush the crust with the beaten egg, sprinkle on sesame seeds, and bake according to the instructions above.

Make-ahead option 2—Freeze the galette: Assemble the galette, but wait to brush with the beaten egg and sprinkle with sesame seeds. Freeze the assembled galette on a baking sheet. Once frozen, remove it from the baking sheet, wrap in foil, and return it to the freezer. When ready to bake, unwrap the galette, brush the crust with the beaten egg, and sprinkle on sesame seeds. Bake according to the instructions above.

SERVES 4

VEGAN: Use vegan butter and omit the salt from the galette dough. Skip the feta. Before baking, brush the crust with almond milk instead of the egg.

For a fun fall gathering, serve this galette with the Wild Rice Harvest Salad on page 59. Make the Chai Poached Pears on page 253 for dessert!

Tofu & Vegetable Green Curry

I love the convenience of premade green curry paste, but rather than buy it in jars, I make my own and freeze it in ice cube trays. With the paste made ahead of time, this curry comes together in a hurry. For a milder curry, use fewer cubes, and of course, for a punchier flavor, use more!

1 tablespoon coconut oil

½ medium yellow onion, chopped

1 cup chopped Japanese or Chinese eggplant

¾ teaspoon sea salt

1 cup chopped broccolini

1 cup sliced red bell pepper

1 cup snow peas

7 ounces extra-firm tofu, cubed

2 (14-ounce) cans full-fat coconut milk

¾ cup Green Curry Paste cubes (3 to 6 cubes, depending on your ice cube tray size, page 151)

Cooked rice (page 71), for serving

Fresh herbs (mint, Thai basil, and/or cilantro), for garnish

Sriracha, for serving

Lime wedges, for serving

Heat the coconut oil in a large pot over medium heat. Add the onion, eggplant, and salt and cook, stirring occasionally, for 5 to 8 minutes, or until softened. Add the broccolini, bell pepper, and snow peas and cook until they begin to soften, about 3 minutes. Add the tofu, coconut milk, and green curry paste cubes and simmer over low heat for 15 minutes, or until the vegetables are tender.

Season to taste, portion into bowls with rice, and garnish with fresh herbs. Serve with sriracha and lime wedges.

recipe continues

SERVES 4

GLUTEN-FREE | VEGAN

GREEN CURRY PASTE CUBES

2½ cups chopped fresh cilantro

8 scallions, chopped

6 garlic cloves

4 serrano peppers, stemmed and chopped

¼ cup coconut oil

3 tablespoons chopped fresh ginger

2 tablespoons fresh lime juice

2 teaspoons lime zest

1½ teaspoons ground cumin

½ teaspoon sea salt

In a food processor, place the cilantro, scallions, garlic, serranos, coconut oil, ginger, lime juice and zest, cumin, and salt. Process until the ingredients are finely chopped and form a thick paste. Portion into 2-tablespoon or ¼-cup ice cube trays and freeze until ready to use.

TIP:

If you have these cubes in your freezer and canned coconut milk in your pantry, you can make green curry any night of the week! I love the curry recipe as written on page 149, but it works well with a variety of other vegetables too. Feel free to swap in what you have on hand. Any of these veggies would be great:

Broccoli

Carrots

Cauliflower

Green beans

Greens (chard, kale, spinach, etc.)

Mushrooms

Potatoes

Sweet potatoes

Zucchini

YIELD: ABOUT 1¼ CUPS

MAKE AHEAD:

To make these burgers in advance, cover the uncooked patties and chill them overnight in the fridge. You can also freeze cooked patties in an airtight container for up to 3 months. To thaw, bake them in a 400°F oven for 10 to 20 minutes, or until heated through.

Sweet Potato Paneer Burgers

These might be my favorite veggie burgers of all time. Creamy sweet potato and sticky brown rice bind them together, little cubes of paneer cheese add richness, and jalapeño and lime juice give them a bright, spicy kick. Since these burgers take some time to prepare, I love to make them in advance. You can chill them in the fridge for up to a day before you cook them, and they also freeze well after they're cooked.

1 large sweet potato

1 bunch scallions, chopped

3 garlic cloves

1 jalapeño pepper, stemmed and diced

2 tablespoons fresh lime juice

1 tablespoon ground turmeric

2 teaspoons grated fresh ginger

1 teaspoon sea salt

½ teaspoon ground cardamom

½ teaspoon ground cumin

2 cups cooked short-grain brown rice* (page 71)

1½ cups panko bread crumbs

3½ ounces paneer, cut into ¼-inch cubes

¼ cup chopped fresh cilantro, plus more for serving

Coconut oil, for the pan

FOR SERVING

¼ cup mayonnaise

1 tablespoon sriracha

8 hamburger buns

Thinly sliced red onions or Pickled Onions (page 78)

SERVES 8

Preheat the oven to 425°F.

Use a fork to poke holes in the sweet potato and place on foil on a baking sheet. Roast for 60 minutes, or until soft. Measure 1 cup of the cooked soft flesh.

In a food processor, place the scallions, garlic, jalapeño, lime juice, turmeric, ginger, salt, cardamom, and cumin. Pulse until the mixture is a roughly chopped paste. Add the 1 cup sweet potato flesh and cooked rice and pulse until combined. Transfer to a large bowl and stir in the panko, paneer, and cilantro until well combined. Form the mixture into 8 patties.

Heat a cast-iron skillet over medium heat. Coat the bottom with oil and cook the burgers for 5 to 6 minutes per side, or until browned and cooked through, working in batches and reducing the heat to low as needed.

In a small bowl, stir together the mayonnaise and sriracha.

Assemble the burgers on the buns with the sriracha mayo, cilantro, and onions.

It's very important that your brown rice is freshly made and sticky so that the burgers will hold together. Because long-grain rice isn't as sticky, be sure to use short-grain rice.

VEGAN: Omit the paneer and use vegan mayo.

THERE ARE TWO WAYS TO MAKE THESE BOWLS IN ADVANCE:

1 Prep each component in advance, but wait to roast the squash until 30 to 40 minutes before serving. Assemble the components inside the spaghetti squash halves and serve.

2 Make the recipe entirely in advance. After roasting the squash, remove the strands. Assemble the bowls in meal prep containers and chill until ready to eat.

Spaghetti Squash Burrito Bowls

You can meal prep these bowls in two different ways. First, you can make the components in advance and serve them with freshly roasted spaghetti squash. Or you can also roast the squash in advance, assemble the bowls in meal prep containers, and enjoy them cold, straight from the fridge. The first option is great for dinner, and the second is perfect for a quick, tasty grab-and-go lunch.

2 medium spaghetti squash (about 2 pounds each)

8 kale leaves, stemmed, leaves roughly chopped

½ teaspoon avocado oil, plus more for drizzling

½ teaspoon fresh lime juice

1 cup cooked black beans, drained and rinsed (page 72)

½ cup fresh cilantro, chopped

Creamy Tomatillo Sauce, chilled (page 76)

½ cup crumbled Cotija cheese

¼ cup pepitas

1 serrano pepper, thinly sliced (optional)

½ cup Pickled Onions (page 78, optional)

Sea salt and freshly ground black pepper

Preheat the oven to 400°F and line a large baking sheet with parchment paper.

Slice the squash in half lengthwise and scoop out the seeds. Drizzle the inside of each half with avocado oil, season with salt and pepper, and place cut side down on the baking sheet. Use a fork to poke holes in the outside of the squash. Roast for 30 to 40 minutes, or until the squash is fork-tender and lightly browned on the edges but still a little bit firm.

In a medium bowl, massage the kale with the avocado oil, lime juice, and a few pinches of salt until the leaves are soft and wilted.

Loosen the spaghetti squash strands with a fork and push them to one side of the squash shells. Assemble the bowls by adding the kale, beans, and cilantro to the shells. Drizzle with some of the chilled tomatillo sauce and top with the cheese, pepitas, serranos, and pickled onions, if using.

SERVES 4

GLUTEN-FREE | VEGAN: Skip the cheese.

To freeze this recipe, let the orzo mixture cool slightly in the baking dish before topping with the panko. Cover and freeze. To reheat, bake, covered, at 425°F for 60 to 90 minutes, or until warmed through. Uncover and broil for 3 to 5 minutes, or until the panko is golden brown.

"Cheesy" Broccoli Bake

If you're someone who likes to take an entire meal out of the freezer and pop it in the oven for dinner, this recipe is for you. "Cheesy" is in quotation marks here because this creamy pasta isn't made with cheese at all. Instead, it uses a vegan-friendly cheese-like sauce made from sweet potato. It's gooey, tangy, and every bit as delicious!

1 large sweet potato, peeled and diced (2 heaping cups)

1 cup water

¼ cup extra-virgin olive oil, plus more for drizzling

1 garlic clove

2 tablespoons nutritional yeast

2 tablespoons tomato paste

1½ teaspoons sea salt, plus more for sprinkling

½ teaspoon onion powder

⅛ teaspoon smoked paprika

1 pound broccoli, small florets plus stems, finely chopped

¾ cup orzo pasta

¼ cup panko bread crumbs

Freshly ground black pepper

Preheat the broiler and oil an 8×8-inch baking dish.

Place the sweet potato in a large saucepan and cover with cold water by about 1 inch. Add a few pinches of salt. Bring to a boil, then reduce the heat and simmer, uncovered, for 8 to 12 minutes, or until fork-tender.

Drain and transfer the sweet potatoes to a high-speed blender. Add the water, olive oil, garlic, nutritional yeast, tomato paste, salt, onion powder, smoked paprika, and several grinds of pepper. Blend until smooth.

Fill the saucepan with more water and bring to a boil. Add the broccoli and boil, uncovered, for 2 minutes. Scoop out the broccoli and set aside. Add some salt to the boiling water and cook the orzo for 6 minutes. It will be slightly underdone, but it will finish cooking in the oven. Drain and transfer the orzo to a large bowl. Add the broccoli and the sauce and stir to combine. Transfer to the prepared baking dish. Sprinkle the panko on top and drizzle with olive oil.

Broil for 3 to 5 minutes, or until the panko is golden brown.

SERVES 4 TO 6

VEGAN

A SIMPLE GUIDE TO
LASAGNA LAYERS

LAYER 4: TOP WITH REMAINING SAUCE + CHEESE

~~~~~~

LAYER 3: HALF THE RICOTTA FILLING + HALF THE VEGETABLES + MORE SAUCE

~~~~~~

LAYER 2: HALF THE RICOTTA FILLING + HALF THE VEGETABLES + MORE SAUCE

~~~~~~

LAYER 1: 1 CUP SAUCE (OR ¼ CUP PESTO) AT THE BOTTOM OF AN OILED 9×13-INCH BAKING DISH

To make lasagna: Follow the guide above using 15 fully cooked lasagna noodles. Bake at 400°F for 30 minutes, or until the cheese is browned and bubbling. Let stand for 20 minutes before garnishing with herbs, slicing, and serving.

For vegan lasagna, use the vegan ricotta on page 161. Skip the cheese and bake, covered, for 25 minutes.

To make ahead: Fully assemble the lasagna in advance. Cover and refrigerate it for up to 4 hours, or freeze for up to 3 months. Transfer a frozen lasagna to the fridge to thaw the day before you plan to serve it. When ready to serve, bake, covered, for 20 minutes. Uncover and bake for 20 to 25 minutes, or until the cheese is browned and bubbling and the lasagna is heated through.

	SPRING	SUMMER	FALL	WINTER
SAUCE	1 heaping cup pesto	24 oz marinara + 2 to 4 tablespoons spicy harissa	1 recipe butternut squash sauce	24 oz marinara sauce
VEGGIES	3 cups fresh spinach + 1 cup peas + 1 (14 oz) can artichoke hearts, drained and chopped	2 small roasted eggplants + 2 roasted zucchini	6 cups torn kale leaves	16 oz roasted mushrooms + 2 roasted fennel bulbs
CHEESE	2 cups grated mozzarella + 2 oz crumbled feta	8 oz torn fresh mozzarella	2 cups grated Gruyère	1½ cups grated mozzarella + 3 oz torn Taleggio
HERBS	chives	basil	parsley	tarragon

SAUCES

BUTTERNUT SQUASH SAUCE

YIELD: ABOUT 2½ CUPS

1 large butternut squash

2 shallots, roughly chopped (⅔ cup)

3 garlic cloves, unpeeled

¼ cup extra-virgin olive oil, plus more for drizzling

¼ cup water

1 teaspoon balsamic vinegar

½ teaspoon sea salt, plus more for sprinkling

Freshly ground black pepper

Preheat the oven to 425°F and line a baking sheet with parchment paper.

Slice the squash in half lengthwise and scoop out the seeds. Drizzle the cut sides with olive oil and sprinkle with salt and pepper. Place cut side down on the baking sheet. Place the shallots and garlic cloves on a piece of foil, drizzle with olive oil and sprinkle with salt, and wrap tightly. Place on the baking sheet and roast for 30 to 45 minutes, or until the squash is soft.

Measure 2 cups of the cooked, soft squash flesh and transfer to a blender with the shallots, peeled garlic, olive oil, water, balsamic vinegar, salt, and several grinds of pepper. Blend until creamy.

MARINARA SAUCE

YIELD: 3 CUPS

2 tablespoons extra-virgin olive oil

1 shallot, finely minced (⅓ cup)

2 large garlic cloves, grated

½ teaspoon sea salt

1 (28-ounce) can crushed tomatoes

2 teaspoons balsamic vinegar

¼ teaspoon cane sugar

¼ teaspoon dried oregano

¼ teaspoon red pepper flakes

Freshly ground black pepper

Heat the olive oil in a medium pot over low heat. Add the shallot, garlic, salt, and several grinds of pepper and cook for 3 minutes, stirring, or until softened.

Add the tomatoes and their juices, the balsamic vinegar, cane sugar, oregano, and red pepper flakes. Cover and simmer over low heat for 20 minutes, stirring occasionally. Season to taste.

PESTO

YIELD: 1 CUP

½ cup pine nuts

2 tablespoons fresh lemon juice

1 small garlic clove

¼ teaspoon sea salt

3 cups fresh basil leaves

½ cup extra-virgin olive oil

Freshly ground black pepper

In a food processor, place the pine nuts, lemon juice, garlic, salt, and several grinds of pepper and pulse until well chopped. Add the basil and pulse until combined. With the food processor running, drizzle in the olive oil and pulse until combined.

ROASTED VEGETABLES

2 small eggplants, cut into ½-inch chunks (about 10 ounces)

2 medium fennel bulbs, chopped

16 ounces cremini mushrooms, stemmed and quartered

2 medium zucchini, cut into ½-inch chunks

For each:

Extra-virgin olive oil, for drizzling

Sea salt and freshly ground black pepper

Preheat the oven to 425°F and line a baking sheet with parchment paper.

Place the vegetables on the baking sheet, drizzle with olive oil, and season with salt and pepper. Toss to coat and spread evenly on the baking sheet. Roast until the vegetables are tender and browned around the edges:

20 to 25 minutes for eggplant

25 to 35 minutes for fennel

15 to 20 minutes for mushrooms

18 to 22 minutes for zucchini

RICOTTA FILLINGS

RICOTTA FILLING

YIELD: 3 CUPS

3 cups (24 ounces) whole milk ricotta cheese

3 garlic cloves, grated

2 teaspoons lemon zest

1 teaspoon sea salt

Freshly ground black pepper

In a large bowl, stir together the ricotta, garlic, lemon zest, salt, and several grinds of pepper.

VEGAN RICOTTA

YIELD: ABOUT 2½ CUPS

14 ounces extra-firm tofu, drained

3 tablespoons fresh lemon juice

2 tablespoons extra-virgin olive oil

2 tablespoons nutritional yeast

1 tablespoon lemon zest

2 garlic cloves

1 teaspoon sea salt

½ teaspoon dried oregano

¼ teaspoon red pepper flakes

In a food processor, place the tofu, lemon juice, olive oil, nutritional yeast, lemon zest, garlic, salt, oregano, and red pepper flakes and pulse until creamy.

3-IN-1

PLANT & PANTRY MEAL PLANS

—

MEAL PREP FOR PEOPLE WHO DON'T LIKE EATING THE SAME THING EVERY DAY

A common misconception about meal prep is that it has to look one way: you line up a bunch of storage containers and you fill them with an identical meal for every day of the week.

While meal prep *can* work like this, it doesn't *have* to.

I, for one, don't always love eating the same thing on repeat. Instead, I like to use leftover components (i.e., a sauce, a cooked grain, or baked tofu) from dinner one night to create a new meal the next. The second meal comes together more quickly because of the prepped components.

You'll find this strategy in these 3-in-1 meal plans.

These 3-day meal plans have a shared grocery list, so you won't end up with tons of leftover ingredients in your fridge at the end.

— **You'll do most of the prep on Day 1.**

— **Leftover components from Day 1 will flow into Days 2 and 3.**

— **You'll cook an entirely different meal each day, but Days 2 and 3 will be streamlined thanks to your Day 1 prep.**

Some plans focus on one type of produce, like zucchini or corn, while others highlight a pantry staple, like rice or beans. They'll all help you find creative ways to transform one set of ingredients into three unique meals.

LET'S GET STARTED

A GARDEN FULL OF

ZUCCHINI

It's the height of summer, and your garden, CSA box, or farmers market haul is overrun with zucchini. How do you use it all up (without baking more zucchini bread)? Easy! Grab some fresh herbs and make these simple recipes.

ALL RECIPES SERVE 4

THE PLAN

RECIPE 1:

Farro Stuffed Zucchini

Make farro filling

Make whipped feta

REUSE ON DAY 3

Prep the zucchini

SAVE THE SCRAP

Stuff zucchini and top with herbs

RECIPE 2:

Zucchini Lemon Pasta

Blend scraps into pasta sauce

Cook the pasta

Sauté zucchini; add pasta and sauce

Top with herbs and nuts

RECIPE 3:

Grilled Zucchini Flatbread

Grill zucchini

Grill flatbread

Spread whipped feta on flatbreads

Assemble with herbs and toppings

TO THE RECIPES

Farro Stuffed Zucchini

FARRO FILLING

1 tablespoon extra-virgin olive oil

1 garlic clove, grated

1 tablespoon fresh lemon juice

½ teaspoon lemon zest

2 cups cooked farro (page 70)

⅓ cup golden raisins

¼ cup kalamata olives, pitted and chopped

2 tablespoons pine nuts

½ teaspoon sea salt

Pinch of red pepper flakes

Freshly ground black pepper

WHIPPED FETA

1 (8-ounce) block feta cheese, crumbled

⅓ cup extra-virgin olive oil

3 tablespoons fresh lemon juice

1 tablespoon water

GRILLED ZUCCHINI

4 medium zucchini

Extra-virgin olive oil, for drizzling

¼ cup fresh basil leaves, torn, for garnish

¼ cup fresh mint leaves, for garnish

Sea salt and freshly ground black pepper

Make the farro filling: In a medium bowl, combine the olive oil, garlic, lemon juice, lemon zest, farro, raisins, olives, pine nuts, salt, red pepper flakes, and several grinds of pepper and toss to coat.

Make the whipped feta: In a food processor, place the feta, olive oil, lemon juice, and water. Pulse until creamy.

Prepare the zucchini: Preheat a grill or grill pan to medium heat. Slice the zucchini in half lengthwise and scoop out the flesh, leaving a ¼-inch-thick shell. Measure 1 cup

of the scooped zucchini flesh and store it in the fridge for Recipe 2. Drizzle the zucchini shells with olive oil and season with salt and pepper. Grill the zucchini cut side down for 3 minutes, or until char marks form. Turn and grill for 2 to 3 more minutes.

Spread 1 heaping tablespoon of the whipped feta into each grilled zucchini shell. Spoon the farro filling into the zucchini, garnish with the basil and mint leaves, and serve. Store the remaining whipped feta in the fridge for Recipe 3.

VEGAN: Replace the whipped feta with vegan ricotta (page 161).

ZUCCHINI SCRAPS AND WHIPPED FETA CARRY OVER TO RECIPES 2 AND 3.

YESTERDAY'S ZUCCHINI SCRAPS BLEND INTO THE CREAMY PASTA SAUCE.

ZUCCHINI RECIPE **2**

Zucchini Lemon Pasta

FOR THE SAUCE

Reserved 1 cup zucchini flesh from Recipe 1

¾ cup raw cashews

¼ cup extra-virgin olive oil

2 tablespoons fresh lemon juice

2 garlic cloves

1 teaspoon sea salt

½ teaspoon Dijon mustard

FOR THE PASTA

10 ounces orecchiette pasta

1 tablespoon extra-virgin olive oil, plus more for drizzling

3 medium zucchini, sliced into coins

¼ cup fresh mint leaves

2 tablespoons chopped fresh dill

2 tablespoons pine nuts

Zest of 1 lemon

Pinch of red pepper flakes

Sea salt and freshly ground black pepper

Make the sauce: Place the reserved zucchini flesh in a high-speed blender with the cashews, olive oil, lemon juice, garlic, salt, and mustard and blend until creamy.

Cook the pasta: Bring a large pot of salted water to a boil. Prepare the pasta according to the package instructions, cooking until al dente. During the last few minutes of cooking, scoop out 1¼ cups of the hot pasta water and set aside. Drain the pasta and toss it with a drizzle of oil to prevent sticking.

Return the pot to the stove. Add the oil, zucchini, and pinches of salt and pepper. Sauté over medium heat for 6 to 8 minutes, or until soft. Stir in the pasta, add the sauce and ½ cup of the reserved pasta water, and toss to combine. Add more pasta water, as needed, if the sauce is too thick. Season to taste.

Portion the pasta into bowls and top with the mint, dill, pine nuts, lemon zest, and red pepper flakes.

GLUTEN-FREE: Use gluten-free pasta.

VEGAN

SAVE EXTRA NUTS AND HERBS FOR RECIPE 3. · · · · · · ·

SLATHER THE FLATBREADS WITH THE REMAINING WHIPPED FETA AND SPRINKLE EXTRA NUTS AND HERBS ON TOP.

ZUCCHINI RECIPE ③

Grilled Zucchini Flatbread

2 zucchini, cut on the bias into ¼-inch-thick slabs

Extra-virgin olive oil, for drizzling

4 store-bought naan

Remaining ¾ cup Whipped Feta (page 166)

Sea salt and freshly ground black pepper

TOPPING OPTIONS

Chopped fresh dill

Chopped kalamata olives

Fresh basil leaves

Fresh mint leaves

Lemon zest

Pine nuts

Red pepper flakes

Preheat a grill or grill pan to medium. Toss the zucchini with drizzles of olive oil and pinches of salt and pepper. Grill for 2 to 3 minutes per side, or until char marks form and the zucchini is tender but still has some bite. Grill the naan for 1 to 2 minutes per side.

Assemble the flatbreads with the whipped feta and grilled zucchini, and sprinkle with desired toppings.

GLUTEN-FREE: Use gluten-free flatbreads.

VEGAN: Replace the whipped feta with vegan ricotta (page 161).

GROCERY LIST
(FOR 3 RECIPES)

PRODUCE

1 medium red cabbage

3 lemons

3 or 4 jalapeño peppers

2 avocados

1 small red onion

1 big bunch fresh cilantro

1 bunch fresh mint

PANTRY & FRIDGE

8 ounces hummus

8 pitas

8 tortillas

2 (14-ounce) cans chickpeas

pepitas

whole milk Greek yogurt

ON HAND

Aleppo pepper or red pepper flakes

apple cider vinegar

extra-virgin olive oil

garlic

ground cardamom

ground cumin

sea salt and black pepper

sesame seeds

A WHOLE HEAD OF
CABBAGE

How many times have you forgotten a hunk of cabbage
at the back of the fridge? I get it! Finishing an entire
cabbage takes planning. Here, I've done that for you.
Get ready to polish one off in 3 days flat!

ALL RECIPES SERVE 4

THE PLAN

RECIPE 1:		RECIPE 2:		RECIPE 3:
Seared Cabbage Wedges		**Loaded Pita Nachos**		**Chickpea Tacos with Pickled Cabbage**

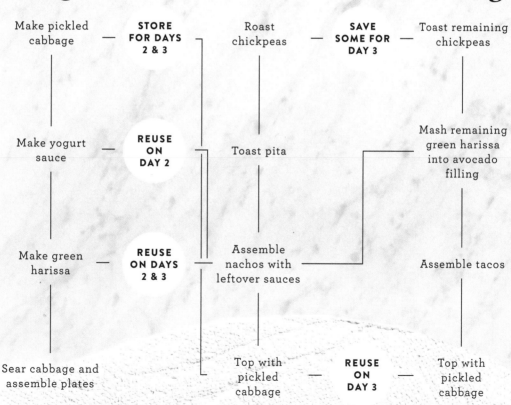

Make pickled cabbage	**STORE FOR DAYS 2 & 3**	Roast chickpeas	**SAVE SOME FOR DAY 3**	Toast remaining chickpeas
Make yogurt sauce	**REUSE ON DAY 2**	Toast pita		Mash remaining green harissa into avocado filling
Make green harissa	**REUSE ON DAYS 2 & 3**	Assemble nachos with leftover sauces		Assemble tacos
Sear cabbage and assemble plates		Top with pickled cabbage	**REUSE ON DAY 3**	Top with pickled cabbage

TO THE RECIPES

CABBAGE RECIPE **1**

Seared Cabbage Wedges

CABBAGE WEDGES

1 medium red cabbage

Extra-virgin olive oil, for drizzling

8 ounces store-bought hummus

1 teaspoon sesame seeds

¼ cup fresh mint leaves

Aleppo pepper or red pepper flakes

2 pitas, halved and warmed, for serving

Sea salt and freshly ground black pepper

YOGURT SAUCE

1 cup whole milk Greek yogurt

4 teaspoons fresh lemon juice

1 tablespoon water, plus more as needed

½ teaspoon sea salt

GREEN HARISSA

3 cups fresh cilantro

½ cup fresh mint leaves

⅓ cup extra-virgin olive oil

¼ cup pepitas

2 tablespoons fresh lemon juice

1 jalapeño pepper, stemmed and chopped

2 garlic cloves

¼ teaspoon ground cardamom

¼ teaspoon ground cumin

¼ teaspoon sea salt

If making the whole series, shred one-quarter of the cabbage and prepare the pickled cabbage on page 176 today. Store the pickled cabbage in the fridge for Recipe 2. Slice the remaining cabbage into 6 equal wedges, keeping the core intact.

Make the yogurt sauce: In a small bowl, stir together the yogurt, lemon juice, water, and salt. If the sauce is too thick, thin with more water to reach a drizzleable consistency.

Make the green harissa: In a food processor, place the cilantro, mint, olive oil, pepitas, lemon juice, jalapeño, garlic, cardamom, cumin, and salt. Pulse until combined.

Heat a cast-iron skillet over high heat. Drizzle the cabbage wedges generously with olive oil, season with salt and pepper, and use your hands to coat them. Sear in the skillet for 8 to 12 minutes per side, or until well charred and blackened, reducing the heat as needed. The middle should be tender when pierced with a knife.

Assemble plates with a slather of the hummus and top each with 1 or 2 cabbage wedges. Drizzle each plate with the yogurt sauce and a heaping tablespoon of the green harissa. Sprinkle with the sesame seeds, mint, and pinches of Aleppo pepper. Serve with the pitas. Store the remaining yogurt sauce and harissa in the fridge for Recipes 2 and 3.

GLUTEN-FREE: Serve with gluten-free pita.

VEGAN: Replace the yogurt sauce with basic cashew cream (page 256). Add water, as needed, to thin the cream to a drizzleable consistency.

GREEN HARISSA AND YOGURT SAUCE CARRY OVER TO RECIPES 2 AND 3. (IF MAKING ALL 3 CABBAGE RECIPES, PREP THE PICKLED CABBAGE FOR DAY 2 ON DAY 1.)

REMEMBER TO PREP YOUR PICKLED CABBAGE A DAY IN ADVANCE!

THE GREEN HARISSA AND YOGURT SAUCE FROM RECIPE 1 BECOME PUNCHY TOPPINGS FOR THESE PITA NACHOS.

CABBAGE RECIPE 2

Loaded Pita Nachos

PICKLED CABBAGE (MAKE AHEAD)

¼ medium red cabbage, shredded (3½ cups)

½ cup thinly sliced red onion

1 cup apple cider vinegar

1 cup water

2 teaspoons sea salt

ROASTED CHICKPEAS

3 cups cooked chickpeas, drained and rinsed (page 72)

Extra-virgin olive oil

Sea salt

TOASTED PITA

6 pitas, cut into wedges

Extra-virgin olive oil

Sea salt

FOR THE NACHOS

Remaining Yogurt Sauce (page 174)

⅓ cup reserved Green Harissa (page 174)

Fresh cilantro leaves

1 jalapeño pepper, sliced

Aleppo pepper or red pepper flakes

One day ahead, make the pickled cabbage: In a large lidded jar, place the cabbage, onion, vinegar, water, and salt. Cover, shake to combine, and chill overnight.

Preheat the oven to 425°F and line three baking sheets with parchment paper.

Roast the chickpeas: Spread the chickpeas on a kitchen towel, pat them dry, and remove any loose skins. Transfer the chickpeas to one of the baking sheets and toss with a drizzle of olive oil and pinches of salt. Roast for 20 to 30 minutes, or until golden brown and crisp.

Toast the pita: Spread the pita on the remaining two baking sheets. Drizzle with olive oil and sprinkle with salt, toss to coat, and spread evenly on the baking sheets. Bake for 13 to 20 minutes, or until crisp, tossing the pita and rotating the pans halfway through.

Make the nachos: Assemble the toasted pita on a platter. Drizzle with the yogurt sauce and dollop with the green harissa. Sprinkle on a heaping ½ cup of the pickled cabbage, ¾ cup of the roasted chickpeas, the cilantro, jalapeños, and pinches of Aleppo pepper. Serve immediately. Store the remaining roasted chickpeas at room temperature for use in Recipe 3. Store the remaining harissa and pickled cabbage in the fridge.

GLUTEN-FREE: Use gluten-free pita.

VEGAN: Replace the yogurt sauce with basic cashew cream (page 256). Add water, as needed, to thin the cream to a drizzleable consistency.

SAVE REMAINING ROASTED CHICKPEAS, GREEN HARISSA, AND PICKLED CABBAGE FOR RECIPE 3.

MASH THE REMAINING GREEN HARISSA WITH AVOCADO TO CREATE A BRIGHT AND CREAMY TACO FILLING.

CABBAGE RECIPE ③

Chickpea Tacos with Pickled Cabbage

Remaining 2¼ cups Roasted Chickpeas (page 176)

2 avocados, diced

Remaining 2 to 3 tablespoons Green Harissa (page 174)

1 tablespoon fresh lemon juice

½ teaspoon sea salt

8 tortillas, warmed

Pickled Cabbage (page 176)

Aleppo pepper or red pepper flakes

1 to 2 jalapeño peppers, sliced

CRISP UP YESTERDAY'S ROASTED CHICKPEAS IN A DRY SKILLET.

Top the tacos with the remaining pickled cabbage for crunch!

Crisp up the chickpeas by adding them to a hot, dry cast-iron skillet. Cook over medium heat, stirring occasionally, for about 5 minutes, or until warm and golden.

In a small bowl, place the avocados, harissa, lemon juice, and salt and use the back of a fork to mash them together.

To assemble the tacos, fill the tortillas with the avocado mixture, roasted chickpeas, pickled cabbage, Aleppo pepper, and jalapeño slices.

GLUTEN-FREE: Use gluten-free tortillas.

VEGAN

GROCERY LIST (FOR 3 RECIPES)

PRODUCE

4 heads broccoli
2 jalapeño peppers
1 bunch scallions
1 daikon radish
microgreens

PANTRY & FRIDGE

8 slices bread
almond milk
dried udon or rice noodles
eggs
provolone cheese
white cheddar cheese

ON HAND

avocado oil
cane sugar
extra-virgin olive oil
fresh ginger
garlic
mayonnaise
red pepper flakes
rice vinegar
tamari
sea salt and black pepper
sesame seeds

BROCCOLI

— AND ITS STEM —

A head of broccoli is like two veggies in one. You've got the
florets, of course, but also the stem. We don't eat the stem as
often, and I wonder why not. It's totally edible and delicious!
Find new ways to use it in this fun, fresh meal plan.

ALL RECIPES SERVE 4

THE PLAN

RECIPE 1:

Broccoli Melts with Broccoli Stem Pickles

RECIPE 2:

Chili Broccoli Noodles

RECIPE 3:

Broccoli Frittata with Everything Left

Make broccoli stem pickles

SAVE ANY EXTRA SCRAPS

Cook the noodles

Whisk eggs with seasonings

Steam florets

Mix noodle ingredients

SAVE REMAINING VEGGIES

Sauté leftover veggies

Bake the melts

Add hot oil and toss noodles

Add the eggs

Top with broccoli stem pickles

REUSE ON DAY 2

Top with broccoli stem pickles

Bake the frittata

TO THE RECIPES

DON'T TOSS THE BROCCOLI STEMS! YOU'LL TURN THEM INTO SWEET AND SPICY PICKLES IN THIS RECIPE.

BROCCOLI RECIPE ❶

Broccoli Melts with Broccoli Stem Pickles

BROCCOLI STEM PICKLES

2 cups julienned broccoli stems
(from 4 heads broccoli)

1 cup julienned daikon radish

1 jalapeño pepper, very thinly sliced

1 cup rice vinegar

1 cup water

3 tablespoons cane sugar

2 teaspoons sea salt

1 garlic clove, smashed

FOR THE MELTS

3 cups small broccoli florets

8 slices bread

Extra-virgin olive oil, for drizzling

1 cup grated white cheddar cheese

4 slices provolone cheese

¼ cup mayonnaise

Sea salt and freshly ground black pepper

Make the pickles: In a large lidded jar, place the broccoli stems, daikon, jalapeño, rice vinegar, water, sugar, salt, and garlic. Cover, shake to combine, and chill for at least 30 minutes.

Make the melts: Preheat the oven to 450°F and line a baking sheet with foil.

Place the broccoli florets in a steamer basket and set over a pot filled with 1 inch of water. Bring the water to a simmer, cover, and steam for 3 minutes. Pat dry.

Place the bread slices on the baking sheet and drizzle with olive oil. Sprinkle the cheddar cheese over 4 of the bread slices, then top with the broccoli florets and the provolone. Bake for 10 minutes, or until the cheese is lightly browned.

Remove from the oven and spread the mayo on the un-topped toasted bread slices. Place a generous scoop (about 2 tablespoons) of the broccoli stem pickles over the broccoli sides. Assemble and serve. Store the remaining pickles in the fridge for Recipe 2.

GLUTEN-FREE: Use gluten-free bread.

SAVE REMAINING BROCCOLI STEM PICKLES FOR RECIPE 2.

TOP THE NOODLES WITH THE
REMAINING BROCCOLI STEM PICKLES
FOR A TANGY POP OF FLAVOR.

BROCCOLI RECIPE **2**

Chili Broccoli Noodles

10 ounces dried udon or rice noodles

2 tablespoons tamari

2 scallions, thinly sliced

2 teaspoons red pepper flakes

1 teaspoon grated fresh ginger

1 garlic clove, grated

⅓ cup avocado oil

Remaining Broccoli Stem Pickles (page 182)

4 soft-boiled eggs, for serving (page 73)

Sesame seeds, for serving

Microgreens, for serving

Bring a large pot of water to a boil.
Prepare the noodles according to the
package instructions. Drain and rinse
under cold water.

In a large heatproof bowl, combine the
tamari, scallions, red pepper flakes,
ginger, and garlic.

In a small saucepan, heat the avocado
oil until it shimmers. Pour the oil over
the red pepper flake mixture and stir to
combine. Add the noodles and toss to
coat.

Portion into bowls and top with the
remaining broccoli stem pickles and the
soft-boiled eggs. Sprinkle with sesame
seeds and microgreens and serve.

GLUTEN-FREE: Use certified gluten-free
rice noodles and tamari.

SAVE ANY REMAINING BROCCOLI, SCALLIONS, AND JALAPEÑO FOR RECIPE 3.

TURN LEFTOVER INGREDIENTS INTO A CLEAN-OUT-THE-FRIDGE FRITTATA!

BROCCOLI RECIPE ❸

Broccoli Frittata with Everything Left

8 large eggs

¼ cup unsweetened almond milk

2 garlic cloves, grated

½ teaspoon sea salt

1 tablespoon extra-virgin olive oil

Remaining scallions, chopped

Remaining broccoli and stem, chopped (about 3 cups)

1 jalapeño pepper, chopped

½ cup grated white cheddar cheese (optional)

Microgreens, for garnish

Freshly ground black pepper

186

Preheat the oven to 400°F.

In a large bowl, whisk together the eggs, almond milk, garlic, salt, and several grinds of pepper. Set aside.

Heat the olive oil in a 10- or 12-inch oven-safe skillet over medium heat. Add the scallions, broccoli, jalapeño, and a pinch of salt and pepper and cook, stirring occasionally, for 5 to 8 minutes, or until the broccoli is tender but still bright green. Pour in the egg mixture and gently shake the pan to distribute. Top with the cheese, if using, and bake for 12 to 20 minutes, or until the eggs are set. Season to taste and serve garnished with microgreens.

GLUTEN-FREE

GROCERY LIST
(FOR 3 RECIPES)

PRODUCE

6 ears fresh corn

4 large poblano peppers

3 medium leeks

2 lemons

1 bunch fresh basil

1 bunch scallions

1 jalapeño pepper

chives

salad greens

PANTRY & FRIDGE

1 (14-ounce) can pinto beans

cornmeal

dry white wine

eggs

panko bread crumbs

pecorino cheese

quick-cooking farro

thick whole milk Greek
yogurt (we like Fage or
Chobani)

white cheddar cheese

ON HAND

avocado oil

extra-virgin olive oil

garlic

onion powder

red pepper flakes

sea salt and black pepper

smoked paprika

whole peppercorns

UP TO YOUR EARS IN

CORN

There's nothing I love more than fresh
summer sweet corn. It's crisp, juicy,
and delectably sweet. When it's in peak
season, I want to eat it every single day.
This meal plan makes it easy!

ALL RECIPES SERVE 4

THE PLAN

RECIPE 1:

Sweet Corn Farrotto

Make broth
with corn and
leek scraps

Make farrotto
with broth
and corn kernels

Season and
serve

RECIPE 2:

Crispy Corn Cakes

Make
yogurt
sauce

Make
corn cakes
with leftover
farrotto

Pan-fry cakes
and serve

RECIPE 3:

Corn Stuffed Poblanos

Roast
the
peppers

Use leftover
corn and sauce
in the filling

Stuff and bake
peppers

**REUSE
ON
DAY 3**

**SAVE
SOME FOR
DAY 2**

TO THE RECIPES

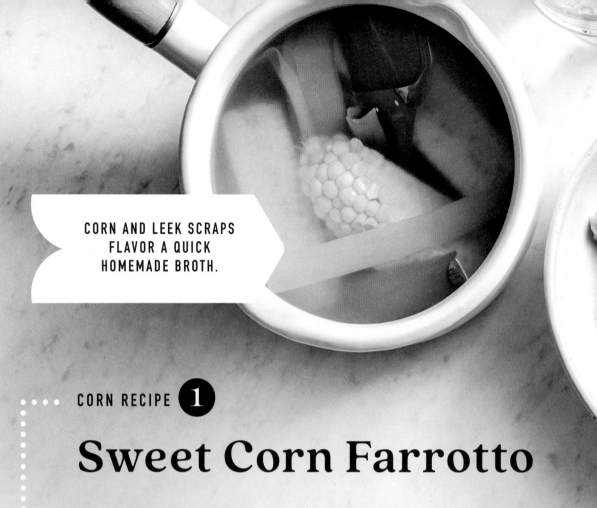

CORN AND LEEK SCRAPS
FLAVOR A QUICK
HOMEMADE BROTH.

CORN RECIPE **1**

Sweet Corn Farrotto

CORN & LEEK SCRAP BROTH

8 cups water

3 to 4 ears corn, husked, kernels removed and reserved (3 cups)

Dark green tops from 3 leeks, washed well

1½ teaspoons sea salt

1½ teaspoons black peppercorns

*There are different types of farro. Seek out quick-cooking, or pearled, farro for this recipe because it requires the shortest time to cook.

FARROTTO

3 tablespoons extra-virgin olive oil

3 leeks, white and light green parts, chopped (about 3½ cups)

5 garlic cloves, chopped

½ teaspoon sea salt

2¼ cups dry quick-cooking farro*

¾ cup dry white wine

6 cups Corn & Leek Scrap Broth

3 cups corn kernels (reserved from broth)

1½ tablespoons fresh lemon juice

1½ teaspoons lemon zest

Pinch of red pepper flakes

Fresh basil leaves, for garnish

Grated pecorino cheese, for serving (optional)

Freshly ground black pepper

Make the broth: In a large pot, combine the water, corncobs, leek tops, salt, and peppercorns. Bring to a boil, cover, reduce the heat, and simmer for 20 minutes. Strain the broth and discard the veggie scraps and peppercorns.

Make the farrotto: Heat the olive oil in a large Dutch oven over medium heat. Add the leeks, garlic, salt, and several grinds of pepper and cook for 5 minutes, or until softened. Stir in the farro and let it cook for 1 minute. Stir in the wine and let it cook down for 30 seconds. Add 2 cups of the broth and simmer, uncovered, for 15 minutes.

Add the corn kernels and 1 more cup of the broth and cook, stirring continuously, for 15 minutes. Add the remaining broth, 1 cup at a time, stirring continuously and allowing each addition of broth to be absorbed by the farro before adding the next. Once all the broth is added, cook until the farrotto is thick and creamy and the farro is tender.

Turn off the heat and stir in the lemon juice, zest, and red pepper flakes. Measure 2 cups of the farrotto and store it in the fridge for Recipe 2. Divide the remaining farrotto among four bowls. Garnish with basil and serve with grated pecorino, if desired.

VEGAN: Skip the cheese.

LEFTOVER FARROTTO WILL TURN INTO CORN CAKES IN RECIPE 2.

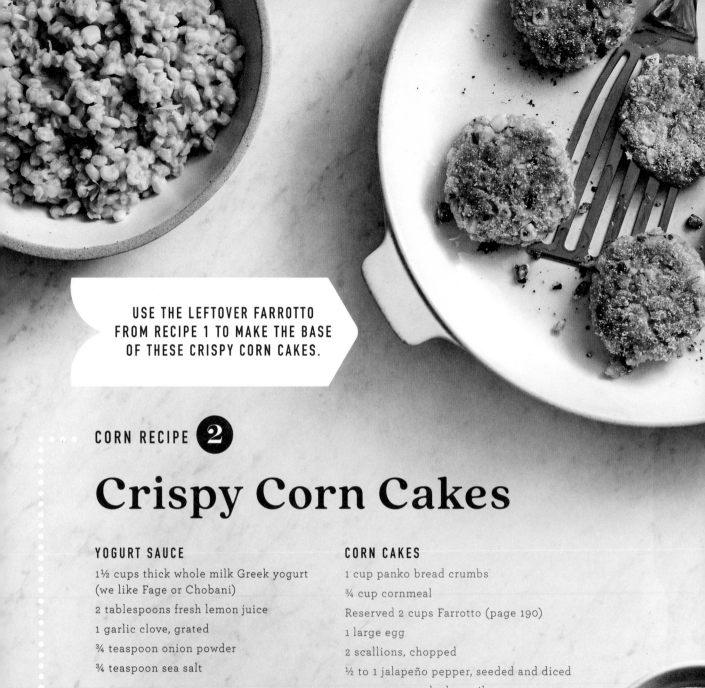

USE THE LEFTOVER FARROTTO FROM RECIPE 1 TO MAKE THE BASE OF THESE CRISPY CORN CAKES.

CORN RECIPE **2**

Crispy Corn Cakes

YOGURT SAUCE

1½ cups thick whole milk Greek yogurt (we like Fage or Chobani)

2 tablespoons fresh lemon juice

1 garlic clove, grated

¾ teaspoon onion powder

¾ teaspoon sea salt

CORN CAKES

1 cup panko bread crumbs

¾ cup cornmeal

Reserved 2 cups Farrotto (page 190)

1 large egg

2 scallions, chopped

½ to 1 jalapeño pepper, seeded and diced

1 teaspoon smoked paprika

¾ teaspoon onion powder

¾ teaspoon sea salt

Avocado oil, for the pan

Salad greens, for serving

Chopped chives, for serving

Freshly ground black pepper

Make the yogurt sauce: In a small bowl, stir together the yogurt, lemon juice, garlic, onion powder, and salt. Store 1 cup of the sauce in the fridge for Recipe 3. Stir a little water into the remaining sauce until it has a dollopable consistency. Chill until ready to serve.

Make the corn cakes: In a shallow bowl, combine ½ cup of the panko with ¼ cup of the cornmeal and set aside. Place the farrotto in a large bowl and add the remaining ½ cup panko and ½ cup cornmeal, the egg, scallions, jalapeño, smoked paprika, onion powder, salt, and several grinds of pepper. Mix until well combined. Use a ¼-cup measuring cup to form the mixture into 10 to 12 patties. Place each into the reserved panko mixture and coat well.

Heat a medium skillet over medium heat. Coat the bottom generously with oil and pan-fry each cake for 2 to 3 minutes per side, or until crisp and golden brown.

Serve the corn cakes with dollops of the yogurt sauce, salad greens, and chives.

VEGAN: In a small bowl, stir together 2 tablespoons ground flaxseed and ¼ cup water. Allow to thicken for 5 minutes, then use in the corn cakes in place of the egg. Make a double batch of the vegan ranch on page 77. Reserve 1 cup for Recipe 3 and serve the remaining vegan ranch with the corn cakes instead of the yogurt sauce.

YOGURT SAUCE CARRIES OVER TO RECIPE 3. ● ● ● ● ● ● ●

Corn Stuffed Poblanos

4 large poblano peppers

Extra-virgin olive oil, for drizzling

Reserved 1 cup Yogurt Sauce (page 192)

1½ cups fresh corn kernels

1¼ cups chopped scallions

1 cup cooked pinto beans, drained and rinsed
(page 72)

1 cup grated white cheddar cheese

½ teaspoon smoked paprika

⅓ cup panko bread crumbs

Chopped chives, for garnish

Red pepper flakes, for garnish

Sea salt and freshly ground black pepper

THE REMAINING YOGURT
SAUCE MAKES THE CORN
FILLING OF THESE STUFFED
PEPPERS RICH AND CREAMY.

Preheat the oven to 475°F. Slice the peppers in half lengthwise, remove the seeds and membranes, and place on a large baking sheet, cut side up. Drizzle with olive oil and sprinkle with salt and pepper and bake for 8 minutes. Tip out and discard any liquid that pools inside the peppers. Set the peppers aside.

In a medium bowl, mix together the yogurt sauce, corn, scallions, pinto beans, cheese, and smoked paprika. Stuff the corn mixture into the pepper halves. Top with the panko, sprinkle with salt, and drizzle generously with olive oil. Bake for 5 minutes, then turn on the broiler and broil for 5 to 10 minutes, or until golden brown. Sprinkle with chives and red pepper flakes and serve.

VEGAN: Skip the cheese and use 1 cup vegan ranch (page 77) plus ¼ teaspoon salt in place of the yogurt sauce. Season the peppers with extra salt and a squeeze of lime after baking.

GROCERY LIST
(FOR 3 RECIPES)

PRODUCE

2 bunches rainbow chard
2 medium leeks
1 bunch curly kale
1 bunch lacinato kale
1 bunch fresh dill
1 pint cherry tomatoes
1 lemon
1 shallot

PANTRY & FRIDGE

32 ounces gnocchi
dried apricots
eggs
pecorino cheese
quick-cooking farro
toasted bread crumbs
(page 257)
walnuts
whole milk ricotta cheese

ON HAND

apple cider vinegar
Dijon mustard
extra-virgin olive oil
garlic
maple syrup
sea salt and black pepper

A FEW BUNCHES OF
GREENS

This feel-good meal plan centers around lush bunches of kale
and rainbow chard. You'll use both the stems and the leaves,
so you'll be eating your pinks and oranges as well as your greens!

ALL RECIPES SERVE 4

THE PLAN

RECIPE 1:	RECIPE 2:	RECIPE 3:
Farro & Greens Gratin	**Kale Pesto Gnocchi**	**Colorful Greens & Grains Salad**

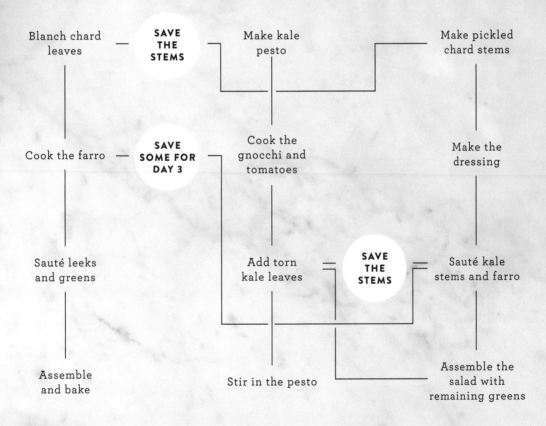

Blanch chard leaves — **SAVE THE STEMS** — Make kale pesto — Make pickled chard stems

Cook the farro — **SAVE SOME FOR DAY 3** — Cook the gnocchi and tomatoes — Make the dressing

Sauté leeks and greens — Add torn kale leaves — **SAVE THE STEMS** — Sauté kale stems and farro

Assemble and bake — Stir in the pesto — Assemble the salad with remaining greens

TO THE RECIPES

Farro & Greens Gratin

2 bunches rainbow chard

1 cup dry quick-cooking farro*

¼ cup extra-virgin olive oil, plus more for the pan

2 leeks, white and light green parts, chopped (3 cups)

½ teaspoon sea salt, plus more for sprinkling

2 garlic cloves, grated

2 large eggs

¼ cup chopped fresh dill

1 teaspoon Dijon mustard

1 cup whole milk ricotta cheese

⅓ cup grated pecorino cheese

1 cup toasted bread crumbs (page 257)

Freshly ground black pepper

*There are different types of farro. Seek out quick-cooking, or pearled, farro for this recipe because it requires the shortest time to cook.

Preheat the oven to 375°F and oil an 8×8-inch baking dish.

Remove the stems from the chard and store them in the fridge for Recipe 3. Bring a large pot of water to a boil, drop in the chard leaves, and blanch for 1 minute. Scoop out the leaves and run under cold water. When cool to the touch, squeeze the excess water out of the leaves and roughly chop. Set aside.

Add the farro to the boiling water and cook for 9 to 11 minutes, or until tender. Drain and measure ¾ cup of the cooked farro for the gratin. Store the remaining farro in the fridge for Recipe 3.

Heat 2 tablespoons of the olive oil in a large skillet over medium heat. Add the leeks, salt, and several grinds of pepper and cook for 5 minutes, or until softened. Stir in the garlic and remove from the heat. Stir in the chard.

In a large bowl, beat the eggs with the dill and mustard. Add the greens mixture, the ¾ cup farro, and the cheeses and fold to combine.

Transfer the mixture to the prepared baking dish and sprinkle the bread crumbs on top. Drizzle with the remaining 2 tablespoons olive oil and sprinkle with salt. Bake for 18 to 20 minutes, or until set.

SAVE LEFTOVER FARRO AND CHARD STEMS FOR RECIPE 3.

GREENS RECIPE **2**

Kale Pesto Gnocchi

1 bunch curly kale

¼ cup walnuts

2 tablespoons fresh lemon juice

1 garlic clove

½ teaspoon sea salt

¼ cup plus 2 tablespoons extra-virgin olive oil

32 ounces store-bought gnocchi

1 pint cherry tomatoes

Freshly ground black pepper

HOLD ON TO THE KALE STEMS! YOU'LL USE THEM IN RECIPE 3.

Remove the stems from the kale and store in the fridge for Recipe 3. Tear the leaves into bite-size pieces.

In a small food processor, place 1½ cups of the kale leaves, the walnuts, lemon juice, garlic, salt, and several grinds of pepper. Pulse until combined, then add ¼ cup of the olive oil and pulse until just combined. The pesto should still be chunky.

Heat the remaining 2 tablespoons olive oil in a large, lidded nonstick skillet over medium heat. Add the gnocchi and cook for 2 minutes without stirring so that it starts to brown on one side. Toss, then cook for

another 2 minutes without stirring. Stir in the tomatoes, cover, and cook for 3 minutes, stirring occasionally.

Reduce the heat to low, add 3 cups of the kale leaves, cover, and cook for 3 more minutes, or until the kale is wilted. Remove from the heat, stir in the pesto, and serve. Store the remaining kale leaves in the fridge for Recipe 3.

GLUTEN-FREE: Use gluten-free gnocchi.

VEGAN: Use vegan gnocchi.

KALE STEMS AND REMAINING LEAVES CARRY OVER TO RECIPE 3. ● ● ● ● ● ●

PULL THE LEFTOVER FARRO, CHARD STEMS, AND KALE STEMS AND LEAVES OUT OF THE FRIDGE. YOU'LL USE THEM ALL IN THIS RECIPE!

The reserved chard stems become vibrant pickles that add color and crunch.

GREENS RECIPE **3**

Colorful Greens & Grains Salad

PICKLED CHARD STEMS

Reserved chard stems from Recipe 1, chopped (about 2 cups)

¼ cup apple cider vinegar

1 teaspoon maple syrup

½ teaspoon sea salt

DRESSING

3 tablespoons apple cider vinegar

2 tablespoons extra-virgin olive oil

1 teaspoon maple syrup

½ teaspoon Dijon mustard

1 garlic clove, grated

½ teaspoon sea salt

Freshly ground black pepper

FOR THE SALAD

1 bunch lacinato kale

Reserved curly kale leaves from Recipe 2

1 tablespoon extra-virgin olive oil

1 shallot, chopped (⅓ cup)

Reserved curly kale stems from Recipe 2, chopped

¼ teaspoon sea salt

Remaining cooked farro (about 2½ cups, page 198)

½ cup chopped dried apricots

½ cup walnuts, chopped

⅓ cup shaved pecorino cheese

THE LEFTOVER FARRO FROM RECIPE 1 MAKES THIS SALAD HEARTY AND SATISFYING.

Make the pickled chard stems: In a lidded jar, place the chopped chard stems, vinegar, maple syrup, and salt. Cover, shake to combine, and chill until ready to use.

Make the dressing: In a small bowl, whisk together the vinegar, olive oil, maple syrup, mustard, garlic, salt, and several grinds of pepper. Set aside.

Make the salad: Remove the stems from the lacinato kale and chop them. Tear the leaves into bite-size pieces. Place the leaves in a large bowl with the reserved curly kale leaves.

Heat the olive oil in a medium skillet over medium heat. Add the shallots, curly and lacinato kale stems, and salt. Cook, stirring, for 5 minutes, or until the kale stems are tender and bright green. Stir in the farro and cook for 1 minute. Remove from the heat and stir in half the dressing.

Add the warm farro mixture to the bowl with the kale leaves and toss. Drain the pickled chard stems and sprinkle on top, along with the dried apricots and walnuts. Toss, then add the remaining dressing and top with the cheese. Season to taste and serve.

VEGAN: Skip the cheese.

GROCERY LIST (FOR 3 RECIPES)

PRODUCE

8 ounces shiitake mushrooms
4 limes
3 baby bok choy
1 English cucumber
1 jalapeño pepper
1 avocado
1 bunch fresh cilantro
1 bunch scallions

PANTRY & FRIDGE

21 ounces extra-firm tofu
frozen shelled edamame
nori sheets
pickled ginger
short-grain brown rice
white miso paste

ON HAND

cane sugar
coconut oil
extra-virgin olive oil
fresh ginger
ground turmeric
mayonnaise
rice vinegar
sea salt
sriracha
tamari

A POT OF

RICE

If you're taking 50 minutes to cook brown rice, why not cook extra?
You can make veggie sushi burritos one day and fried rice the next.
Then, polish it off with a zesty miso soup!

ALL RECIPES SERVE 4

First, cook the rice

RECIPE 1:	RECIPE 2:	RECIPE 3:
Veggie Sushi Burritos	**Cilantro Lime Fried Rice**	**Brown Rice Miso Mushroom Soup**

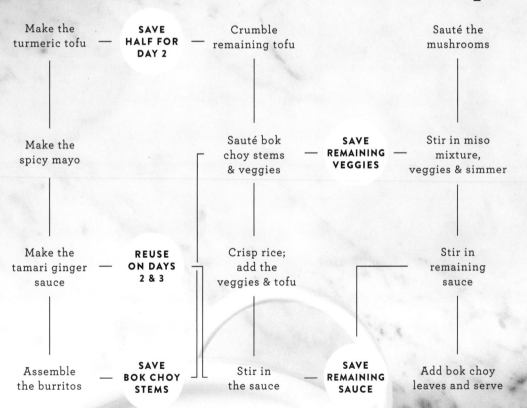

Make the turmeric tofu — **SAVE HALF FOR DAY 2** — Crumble remaining tofu

Sauté the mushrooms

Make the spicy mayo

Sauté bok choy stems & veggies — **SAVE REMAINING VEGGIES** — Stir in miso mixture, veggies & simmer

Make the tamari ginger sauce — **REUSE ON DAYS 2 & 3** — Crisp rice; add the veggies & tofu

Stir in remaining sauce

Assemble the burritos — **SAVE BOK CHOY STEMS** — Stir in the sauce — **SAVE REMAINING SAUCE** — Add bok choy leaves and serve

TO THE RECIPES ● ● ● ● ● ● ● ●

FIRST, COOK THE RICE

3 cups dry short-grain brown rice, rinsed well

6 cups water

2 teaspoons extra-virgin olive oil

Combine the rice, water, and olive oil in a large pot or Dutch oven and bring to a boil. Cover, reduce the heat, and simmer for 45 minutes, or until the water is absorbed. Remove from the heat and let sit, covered, for 10 minutes. Fluff with a fork.

Use 4 cups freshly cooked rice in Recipe 1. Store the remaining rice in the fridge for Recipes 2 and 3.

USE 4 CUPS FRESHLY COOKED RICE IN RECIPE 1. SAVE REMAINING RICE FOR RECIPES 2 AND 3.

RICE RECIPE ①

Veggie Sushi Burritos

TURMERIC TOFU

½ cup rice vinegar

2 teaspoons ground turmeric

1½ teaspoons sea salt

14 ounces extra-firm tofu, patted dry
and cut into long ¼-inch-thick strips

SPICY MAYO

¼ cup mayonnaise

1 tablespoon sriracha

TAMARI GINGER SAUCE

½ cup tamari

¼ cup fresh lime juice

¼ cup rice vinegar

2 tablespoons cane sugar

½ teaspoon grated fresh ginger

¼ cup water

FOR THE SUSHI BURRITOS

4 nori sheets

4 cups freshly cooked short-grain
brown rice (page 207)

Leaves from 2 baby bok choy

½ English cucumber, sliced into long strips

1 jalapeño pepper, sliced into thin strips

1 large avocado, sliced into thin strips

Pickled ginger

Make the turmeric tofu: Preheat the oven to 425°F and line a baking sheet with parchment paper. In a shallow dish, stir together the vinegar, turmeric, and salt. Add the tofu, toss to coat, and let marinate for 5 minutes. Place the tofu on the prepared baking sheet. Bake for 20 minutes, or until browned around the edges. Once cooled, store half the tofu in the fridge for Recipe 2.

Make the spicy mayo: In a small bowl, stir together the mayo and sriracha.

Make the tamari ginger sauce: In a small bowl, stir together the tamari, lime juice, vinegar, sugar, and ginger. Store ⅔ cup of the mixture in the fridge for Recipes 2 and 3. Add the water to the remaining mixture in the bowl and set aside to use as a dipping sauce.

Assemble the sushi burritos: Place one nori sheet, glossy side down, on your work space. Dampen your fingers with a little water and press 1 cup of the rice evenly onto the sheet, leaving 1 inch at the top and bottom for sealing. In the center of the rice, horizontally arrange a few of the bok choy leaves, tofu strips, cucumber strips, jalapeño strips, avocado strips, and pickled ginger. Drizzle the filling with the spicy mayo. Starting at the bottom edge of the nori, tuck and roll the sushi burrito closed.

Repeat to assemble the remaining burritos and serve with the dipping sauce.

GLUTEN-FREE: Use certified gluten-free tamari.

VEGAN: Use vegan mayo.

BOK CHOY STEMS, TURMERIC TOFU, AND TAMARI GINGER SAUCE CARRY OVER TO RECIPES 2 AND 3.

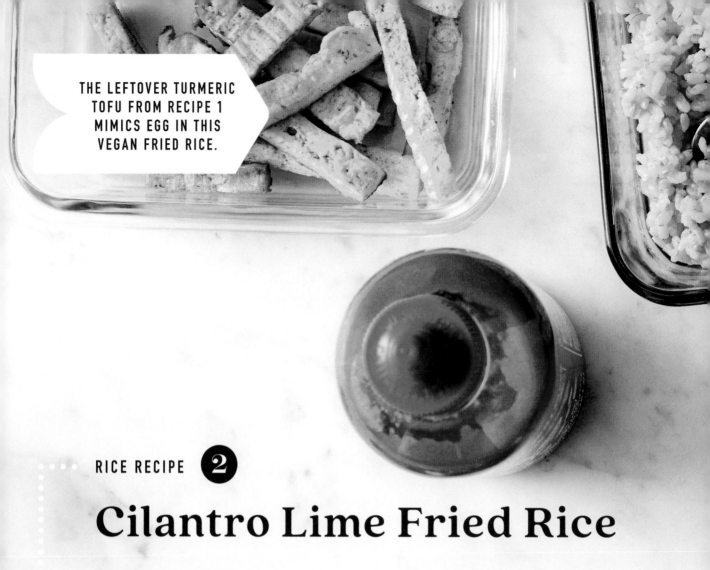

THE LEFTOVER TURMERIC TOFU FROM RECIPE 1 MIMICS EGG IN THIS VEGAN FRIED RICE.

RICE RECIPE **2**

Cilantro Lime Fried Rice

1 tablespoon coconut oil

1 bunch scallions, chopped
(reserve ⅓ cup for Recipe 3)

Stems from 2 baby bok choy, chopped

1 bunch fresh cilantro, stems finely
chopped, leaves reserved for garnish

¼ teaspoon sea salt

3 cups leftover cooked brown rice (page 207)

Reserved Turmeric Tofu, crumbled (page 208)

¾ cup frozen shelled edamame, thawed

⅓ cup reserved Tamari Ginger Sauce
(page 208)

Sriracha, for serving

CHOP THE
RESERVED BOK
CHOY STEMS TO
ADD A VEGGIE
PUNCH.

Heat 1 teaspoon of the coconut oil in a large nonstick skillet over medium heat. Add the scallions, bok choy stems, cilantro stems, and salt and cook for 1 minute. Remove from the pan and set aside.

Heat the remaining 2 teaspoons coconut oil in the skillet over medium heat. Add the rice, press it into a single layer at the bottom of the pan, and cook without stirring for 6 to 8 minutes, or until the rice is lightly crisp on the bottom. Stir, then add the veggies back to the pan, along with the tofu and edamame. Cook for 2 minutes, or until warmed through. Stir in the tamari ginger sauce and season to taste. Garnish with the cilantro leaves and serve with sriracha. Store the remaining tamari ginger sauce and reserved scallions in the fridge for Recipe 3.

GLUTEN-FREE: Use certified gluten-free tamari.

VEGAN

SAVE A FEW CHOPPED SCALLIONS AND THE REMAINING TAMARI GINGER SAUCE FOR RECIPE 3.

USE UP YOUR RICE, SCALLIONS, AND TAMARI GINGER SAUCE IN THIS NOURISHING, SAVORY SOUP.

RICE RECIPE 3

Brown Rice Miso Mushroom Soup

1 tablespoon coconut oil

8 ounces shiitake mushrooms, stemmed and sliced

4 cups water

⅓ cup white miso paste

⅓ cup reserved chopped scallions from Recipe 2

1 baby bok choy, stems and leaves chopped, leaves reserved

7 ounces extra-firm tofu, patted dry and cut into 1-inch cubes

½ cup frozen shelled edamame, thawed

Remaining 2 cups cooked brown rice (page 207)

Remaining ⅓ cup Tamari Ginger Sauce (page 208)

Heat the coconut oil in a large pot or Dutch oven over medium heat. Add the mushrooms and cook, stirring occasionally, for 5 to 8 minutes, or until softened.

Add the water and stir. Bring to a gentle simmer, then scoop ⅔ cup of the water into a small bowl. Add the miso paste and whisk vigorously to combine. Stir the miso mixture back into the pot and add the scallions, bok choy stems, tofu, edamame, rice, and tamari ginger sauce. Simmer gently over very low heat for 5 minutes.

Add the bok choy leaves and stir until wilted. Season to taste and serve.

GLUTEN-FREE: Use certified gluten-free tamari.

VEGAN

GROCERY LIST (FOR 3 RECIPES)

PRODUCE

8 medium tomatoes

4 cups arugula

2 lemons

1 bunch fresh basil

1 bunch fresh parsley

1 pint cherry tomatoes

PANTRY & FRIDGE

1 (24-ounce) jar marinara sauce (we like Rao's)

French green lentils

hazelnuts

lasagna noodles

nutritional yeast

pecorino cheese

sourdough bread

whole milk ricotta cheese

ON HAND

dried oregano

extra-virgin olive oil

garlic

red pepper flakes

sea salt and black pepper

A BATCH OF

LENTILS

Packed with fiber and protein, lentils are a plant-based powerhouse. Cook a pot on the weekend, and use them in fresh, summery bowls, the cutest stuffed tomatoes, and a quick stovetop lasagna during the week.

ALL RECIPES SERVE 4

First, cook the lentils

RECIPE 1:	RECIPE 2:	RECIPE 3:
# Tomato Lentil Bowls	# Lentil Stuffed Tomatoes	# Lentil Skillet Lasagna

Make the hazelnut bread crumbs — **REUSE ON DAYS 2 & 3** — Make the filling

Cook the noodles in marinara

Make the lemon ricotta — **REUSE ON DAY 3** — Stuff the tomatoes

Fold in the lentils and arugula

Assemble the bowls

Bake the tomatoes

Serve with lemon ricotta

Sprinkle with bread crumbs

TO THE RECIPES

FIRST, COOK THE LENTILS

Heaping 1½ cups dry French green lentils, rinsed

Place the lentils in a medium pot of water and bring to a boil. Reduce the heat and simmer, uncovered, stirring occasionally, for 17 to 20 minutes, or until tender but not mushy. Drain and let cool.

Use 2 cups cooked lentils in Recipe 1. Store the remaining lentils in the fridge for Recipes 2 and 3.

USE 2 CUPS COOKED LENTILS IN RECIPE 1.
SAVE REMAINING LENTILS FOR RECIPES 2 AND 3.

LENTILS RECIPE ①

Tomato Lentil Bowls

HAZELNUT BREAD CRUMBS

4 cups roughly chopped sourdough bread

1 cup hazelnuts

¼ cup nutritional yeast

1 teaspoon sea salt

½ teaspoon red pepper flakes

½ teaspoon dried oregano

LEMON RICOTTA

16 ounces whole milk ricotta cheese

1 tablespoon lemon zest

½ teaspoon sea salt

Freshly ground black pepper

FOR THE BOWLS

2 cups cooked lentils (page 217)

½ cup finely chopped fresh parsley

2 garlic cloves, grated

2 tablespoons fresh lemon juice, plus more for squeezing

1 tablespoon extra-virgin olive oil, plus more for drizzling

½ teaspoon sea salt

1 pint cherry tomatoes, halved

2 cups arugula

Fresh basil leaves

Freshly ground black pepper

Preheat the oven to 350°F and line two baking sheets with parchment paper.

Make the hazelnut bread crumbs: In a food processor, place the bread and pulse a few times until coarsely ground, with some larger chunks still remaining. Spread onto one of the baking sheets and bake for 10 to 18 minutes, or until crisp and lightly browned, tossing halfway through.

Spread the hazelnuts on the second baking sheet and bake for 10 minutes, or until fragrant. Transfer to the food processor and add the nutritional yeast, salt, red pepper flakes, and oregano. Pulse until the hazelnuts are coarsely chopped. Transfer to a bowl and stir in the bread crumbs. Store 2 cups of the mixture at room temperature for Recipes 2 and 3.

Make the lemon ricotta: In a medium bowl, stir together the ricotta, lemon zest, salt, and several grinds of pepper. Store half the mixture in the fridge for Recipe 3.

Make the bowls: In a medium bowl, combine the lentils, parsley, garlic, lemon juice, olive oil, salt, and several grinds of pepper.

Assemble the bowls with a swoosh of the lemon ricotta, the lentil mixture, the tomatoes, and arugula. Sprinkle with the remaining bread crumbs and fresh basil. Drizzle with a little olive oil, squeeze with lemon juice, and season to taste.

GLUTEN-FREE: Use gluten-free bread.

VEGAN: Replace the lemon ricotta with vegan ricotta (page 161).

HAZELNUT BREAD CRUMBS AND LEMON RICOTTA CARRY OVER TO RECIPES 2 AND 3.

LEFTOVER LENTILS CREATE THE FILLING FOR THESE STUFFED TOMATOES.

LENTILS RECIPE ❷

Lentil Stuffed Tomatoes

1 cup cooked lentils (page 217)

1 cup reserved Hazelnut Bread Crumbs (page 218)

¼ cup finely chopped fresh basil leaves, plus more for garnish

¼ cup finely chopped fresh parsley

1 teaspoon lemon zest

¼ teaspoon sea salt, plus more for sprinkling

½ cup grated pecorino cheese

8 medium tomatoes

Extra-virgin olive oil, for drizzling

Freshly ground black pepper

THE HAZELNUT BREAD CRUMBS FROM RECIPE 1 ADD FLAVOR AND TEXTURE TO THE FILLING.

Preheat the oven to 375°F.

In a large bowl, combine the lentils, bread crumbs, basil, parsley, lemon zest, salt, and 2 tablespoons of the pecorino.

Slice ½ inch off the top of each tomato and scoop out the flesh. Place the tomatoes in a baking dish, season the insides with salt and pepper, and spoon in the filling. Sprinkle the filled tomatoes with the remaining pecorino and drizzle with a little olive oil. Bake for 30 minutes, or until the topping is lightly golden brown. If desired, roast the tomato tops on a baking sheet alongside the tomatoes.

Garnish with fresh basil and serve.

GLUTEN-FREE: Make the bread crumbs with gluten-free bread.

VEGAN: Skip the cheese and season the tomatoes with extra salt after baking.

SAVE REMAINING HAZELNUT BREAD CRUMBS FOR RECIPE 3.

Lentil Skillet Lasagna

2 tablespoons extra-virgin olive oil

1 (24-ounce) jar store-bought marinara sauce (we like Rao's)

1½ cups water

10 ounces lasagna noodles, broken into four pieces each

2 cups arugula

Remaining 1 cup cooked lentils (page 217)

Remaining 1 cup Lemon Ricotta (page 218)

Fresh basil leaves, for garnish

Remaining 1 cup Hazelnut Bread Crumbs (page 218)

FINISH UP YOUR COOKED LENTILS IN THIS EASY STOVETOP LASAGNA RECIPE.

222

Serve the lasagna with dollops of the leftover lemon ricotta and sprinkle it with hazelnut bread crumbs for crunch.

Heat the olive oil in a large, deep lidded skillet over medium heat. Add the marinara sauce and water and cook for 2 minutes, or until heated through. Stir in the lasagna noodles, cover, and simmer over low heat, stirring occasionally, for 15 to 20 minutes, or until the noodles are al dente.

Fold in the arugula and lentils and stir until the arugula is wilted. Remove from the heat. Serve with dollops of the ricotta, fresh basil, and the remaining bread crumbs on the side.

GLUTEN-FREE: Use gluten-free pasta and make the bread crumbs with gluten-free bread.

VEGAN: Replace the lemon ricotta with vegan ricotta (page 161).

PRODUCE

3 lemons

3 medium carrots

2 fennel bulbs with stalks

2 shallots

1 bunch curly kale

1 bunch fresh parsley

1 bunch fresh tarragon

1 bunch fresh thyme

1 head radicchio

1 navel orange

PANTRY & FRIDGE

1 (14-ounce) can artichoke hearts

capers

dry great northern beans

jarred roasted red peppers

orzo pasta

pecorino cheese

pine nuts

ON HAND

Dijon mustard

extra-virgin olive oil

garlic

red pepper flakes

sea salt and black pepper

A POT OF

BEANS

Cooking beans from scratch takes time, but if
you ask me, every second is worth it. The beans
themselves are far more flavorful than the canned
ones, and their cooking broth is also delicious.
Use both in this simple meal plan!

ALL RECIPES SERVE 4

THE PLAN

First, cook the beans and their fennel top broth

RECIPE 1:

Radicchio & White Bean Salad

Make the lemon artichoke white beans

SAVE SOME FOR DAY 2

Be sure to save bean cooking broth

Add remaining salad ingredients and serve

RECIPE 2:

Braised Fennel with White Beans

Sear fennel wedges

Add lemon artichoke beans with bean cooking broth

Cover and bake

Make and sprinkle herb topping

RECIPE 3:

White Bean Orzo Soup

Sauté veggies

Add remaining beans and broth

Simmer the soup

Add more veggies and lemon

TO THE RECIPES

CAN I USE CANNED BEANS?

Readers commonly ask me if they can use canned beans in a recipe instead of dried ones. Oftentimes you can, but not in this series! These recipes are all about the beans and their cooking broth, so make sure to cook the beans from scratch.

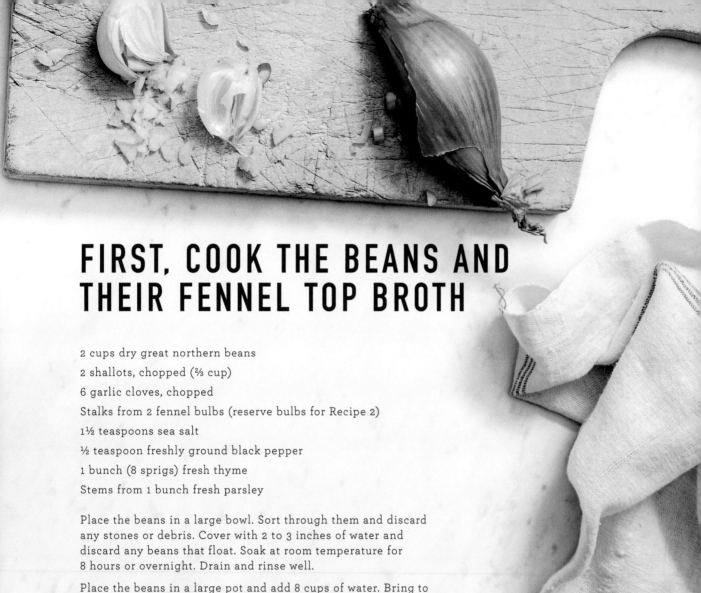

FIRST, COOK THE BEANS AND THEIR FENNEL TOP BROTH

2 cups dry great northern beans

2 shallots, chopped (⅔ cup)

6 garlic cloves, chopped

Stalks from 2 fennel bulbs (reserve bulbs for Recipe 2)

1½ teaspoons sea salt

½ teaspoon freshly ground black pepper

1 bunch (8 sprigs) fresh thyme

Stems from 1 bunch fresh parsley

Place the beans in a large bowl. Sort through them and discard any stones or debris. Cover with 2 to 3 inches of water and discard any beans that float. Soak at room temperature for 8 hours or overnight. Drain and rinse well.

Place the beans in a large pot and add 8 cups of water. Bring to a boil and skim off any foam that rises to the surface. Reduce the heat, then add the shallots, garlic, fennel stalks, salt, and pepper. Use kitchen twine to tie the thyme and parsley stems together and add the bundle to the pot. Simmer, uncovered, for 1 hour, stirring occasionally. Add 2 more cups of water and continue simmering for 30 to 60 minutes, or until the beans are tender. The timing will depend on the freshness of your beans. (Older beans will take longer than fresher ones.)

When the beans are tender, remove and discard the thyme, parsley stems, and fennel stalks.

Use a slotted spoon to scoop out 4 cups cooked beans for Recipe 1. Store the remaining beans and their cooking broth in the fridge for Recipes 2 and 3.

USE 4 CUPS BEANS IN RECIPE 1. SAVE THE REMAINING BEANS AND BROTH FOR RECIPES 2 AND 3. SAVE THE FENNEL BULBS FOR RECIPE 2.

Radicchio & White Bean Salad

LEMON ARTICHOKE WHITE BEANS

4 cups cooked white beans (page 227)

1 (14-ounce) can artichoke hearts, drained and chopped

2 jarred roasted red peppers, chopped

¼ cup extra-virgin olive oil

2 tablespoons capers

2 tablespoons fresh lemon juice

1 teaspoon Dijon mustard

½ teaspoon sea salt

Freshly ground black pepper

FOR THE SALAD

3 radicchio leaves, thinly sliced

½ cup chopped fresh parsley

1 tablespoon fresh orange juice

Shaved pecorino cheese (optional)

Make the lemon artichoke white beans: In a large bowl, combine the beans, artichoke hearts, red peppers, olive oil, capers, lemon juice, mustard, salt, and several grinds of pepper. Stir to coat. Store 2¼ cups of the lemon artichoke beans in the fridge for Recipe 2.

Make the salad: Add the radicchio, parsley, and orange juice to the remaining bean mixture and toss to coat. Season to taste and serve with shaved pecorino, if desired.

GLUTEN-FREE

VEGAN: Skip the cheese.

LEMON ARTICHOKE WHITE BEANS CARRY OVER TO RECIPE 2.

THE LEMON ARTICHOKE WHITE BEANS FROM RECIPE 1 CREATE A FLAVORFUL BASE FOR THIS ONE-PAN MEAL. YOU'LL USE THE RESERVED FENNEL BULBS AND SOME OF THE BEAN COOKING BROTH HERE TOO!

BEANS RECIPE ②

Braised Fennel with White Beans

2 reserved fennel bulbs from cooking the beans (page 227)

1 tablespoon extra-virgin olive oil

Reserved 2¼ cups Lemon Artichoke White Beans (page 228)

¾ cup reserved bean cooking broth (page 227)

Lemon wedge, for squeezing

Sea salt and freshly ground black pepper

TOPPING

⅓ cup chopped fresh parsley

⅓ cup pine nuts, chopped

1 tablespoon chopped fresh tarragon

1 tablespoon lemon zest

1 tablespoon orange zest

⅛ teaspoon sea salt

Pinch of red pepper flakes (optional)

Preheat the oven to 425°F.

Slice each fennel bulb into 8 wedges, keeping the core intact. Heat the olive oil in a 10-inch cast-iron skillet over medium heat. Working in batches if necessary, place the fennel wedges into the pan and sear for 3 to 4 minutes per side, or until browned. Remove the fennel from the pan and turn off the heat.

Add the reserved lemon artichoke beans and the bean cooking broth to the skillet and spread the beans in an even layer. Nestle the fennel wedges on top. Cover the skillet with a lid or foil, transfer to the oven, and bake for 25 minutes, or until the fennel is tender.

Make the topping: In a small bowl, stir together the parsley, pine nuts, tarragon, lemon zest, orange zest, salt, and red pepper flakes, if using.

Carefully remove the skillet from the oven, uncover, and let sit for 10 minutes. Squeeze lemon juice over the fennel, season with salt and pepper, sprinkle with the topping, and serve.

GLUTEN-FREE

VEGAN

SAVE REMAINING BEANS AND BROTH FOR RECIPE 3.

USE THE REMAINING
BEANS AND BROTH IN
THIS EASY SOUP.

BEANS RECIPE ❸

White Bean Orzo Soup

2 tablespoons extra-virgin olive oil

3 medium carrots, chopped

2 curly kale leaves, stems chopped,
leaves torn

½ teaspoon sea salt

Remaining 2 cups cooked white beans
(page 227)

Remaining 3½ cups bean cooking broth
(page 227)

1 cup water, plus more if needed

¾ cup orzo pasta

1 jarred roasted red pepper, chopped

1 tablespoon fresh lemon juice

¼ cup chopped fresh parsley

1 tablespoon chopped fresh tarragon

Grated pecorino cheese, for serving (optional)

Freshly ground black pepper

Heat the olive oil in a large pot over medium heat. Add the carrots, kale stems, salt, and several grinds of pepper and cook for 4 minutes, or until softened. Add the beans, the bean cooking broth, and the water and simmer for 15 minutes. Add the orzo and simmer for 8 minutes.

Stir in the red pepper, lemon juice, and kale leaves and cook for 2 minutes, or until the kale is wilted. If the soup is too thick, add ½ cup more water. Stir in the parsley and tarragon and serve with grated pecorino cheese, if desired.

GLUTEN-FREE: Use gluten-free pasta.

VEGAN: Skip the cheese.

DESSERT

Strawberry Polenta Cake

This lemony polenta cake is the perfect treat to share at a summer gathering. Topped with toasted almonds and ruby red strawberries, it looks impressive, but it's delightfully simple to make. The moist, tender cake is wonderful on its own, but you could certainly dress it up more with a scoop of vanilla ice cream or a dusting of powdered sugar.

1 cup all-purpose flour, spooned and leveled (see page 23)

½ cup medium-grind cornmeal, spooned and leveled (see page 23)

2 teaspoons baking powder

¾ teaspoon sea salt

½ cup cane sugar

1 tablespoon lemon zest

¾ cup whole milk Greek yogurt

½ cup extra-virgin olive oil, plus more for the pan

2 large eggs

1 teaspoon vanilla extract

½ teaspoon almond extract

1½ cups small strawberries, halved

¼ cup sliced almonds

Preheat the oven to 350°F. Lightly oil a 9-inch round cake pan and line the bottom of the pan with parchment paper.

In a medium bowl, whisk together the flour, cornmeal, baking powder, and salt.

In a large bowl, whisk together the sugar and lemon zest. Add the yogurt, olive oil, eggs, vanilla, and almond extract and whisk to combine.

Add the dry ingredients to the wet ingredients and stir until just combined. Don't overmix.

Pour the batter into the prepared pan and top with the strawberries and almonds. Bake for 35 to 40 minutes, or until a toothpick inserted in the center comes out clean. Let cool completely before slicing and serving.

SERVES 8

Zucchini Snack Cake

This cute little cake never lasts long in our house. It's just the right amount of sweet, but not too sweet, so you can swipe a slice for an afternoon snack (or even breakfast) and then circle back later for dessert. The zucchini and almond flour make it super moist, and the walnuts and oats add a nice crunch on top. It keeps well in an airtight container at room temperature for up to 3 days. In the unlikely event that you have some left after that, pop it in the freezer. It'll thaw perfectly for a treat down the road.

1 cup all-purpose flour, spooned and leveled (see page 23)

½ cup almond flour, spooned and leveled (see page 23)

1 teaspoon baking powder

1 teaspoon cinnamon .

½ teaspoon baking soda

½ teaspoon nutmeg

½ teaspoon sea salt

½ cup extra-virgin olive oil

½ cup cane sugar

2 large eggs

Zest of 1 lemon

1 teaspoon vanilla extract

2 cups shredded zucchini (about 2 medium)*

¼ cup chopped walnuts

2 tablespoons whole rolled oats

Preheat the oven to 350°F and line an 8×8-inch baking dish with parchment paper.

In a medium bowl, whisk together the flour, almond flour, baking powder, cinnamon, baking soda, nutmeg, and salt.

In a large bowl, whisk together the olive oil, sugar, eggs, lemon zest, and vanilla.

Add the dry ingredients to the wet ingredients and stir until just combined. Fold in the zucchini. The batter will be thick.

Pour the batter into the prepared baking dish and use a spatula to evenly spread it to the edges of the pan. Sprinkle the walnuts and oats on top and bake for 34 to 36 minutes, or until a toothpick inserted in the center comes out clean.

No need to squeeze or pat the moisture out of the shredded zucchini.

SERVES 12

Needless to say, a scoop of vanilla ice cream only makes this recipe better.

Summer Fruit Cobbler

When summer fruits like peaches and berries are at their peak, you don't have to do much to turn them into a delicious dessert. Here, I toss them with a little sugar and cornstarch to make a juicy, jammy cobbler filling. A thin layer of biscuits offers a nice rich contrast to the fruit without overwhelming it.

BISCUIT TOPPING

1 cup all-purpose flour, spooned and leveled, plus more for rolling (see page 23)

¼ cup plus 2 tablespoons almond flour, spooned and leveled (see page 23)

2½ tablespoons cane sugar

1¼ teaspoons baking powder

½ teaspoon cinnamon

Heaping ¼ teaspoon sea salt

4 tablespoons cold unsalted butter, cut into small pieces, plus more for the skillet

1 large egg, beaten

1 tablespoon almond milk, plus more for brushing

Coarse sugar, for sprinkling (optional)

FRUIT FILLING

3 peaches, pitted and sliced

1 cup blackberries

1 cup raspberries

2 tablespoons cane sugar

4 teaspoons cornstarch

1 teaspoon cinnamon

Preheat the oven to 400°F and grease an enameled 10-inch cast-iron skillet or similar baking dish.

Make the topping: In a medium bowl, whisk together the flour, almond flour, sugar, baking powder, cinnamon, and salt. Using your hands, work in the butter until the mixture resembles coarse sand. Add the egg and almond milk and fold to form a shaggy dough. Use your hands to form it into a ball.

Turn the dough out onto a lightly floured piece of parchment paper and roll into a ½-inch-thick rectangle. Place on a baking sheet and freeze while you prepare the filling.

Make the filling: In a medium bowl, combine the peaches, berries, sugar, cornstarch, and cinnamon and toss to coat the fruit. Scoop the filling into the prepared skillet.

Remove the biscuit dough from the freezer and use a 2¼-inch round biscuit cutter to cut out 9 to 10 biscuits, rerolling the scraps as necessary. Arrange the biscuits evenly on top of the fruit filling.

Brush the tops of the biscuits with a little almond milk and sprinkle with coarse sugar, if using.

Bake for 25 to 30 minutes, or until the fruit is bubbling and the biscuits are golden brown.

SERVES 6

Vegan Chocolate Banana Bread

Chocolate lovers, this one's for you! This vegan banana
bread is amazingly moist and fudgy, and you can mix up the
batter in under 15 minutes. Enjoy a thick slice for dessert,
or serve it as an afternoon treat with a cup of coffee or tea.

1 cup mashed very ripe banana
(about 2 large)

½ cup plus 2 tablespoons almond milk

½ cup cane sugar

¼ cup extra-virgin olive oil, plus more for
the pan

1 teaspoon vanilla extract

¾ cup all-purpose flour, spooned and leveled
(see page 23)

¾ cup whole wheat flour, spooned and
leveled (see page 23)

½ cup almond flour, spooned and leveled
(see page 23)

⅓ cup unsweetened cocoa powder

2 teaspoons baking powder

½ teaspoon cinnamon

½ teaspoon sea salt

¼ teaspoon baking soda

¼ teaspoon nutmeg

⅓ cup dark chocolate chips

Preheat the oven to 350°F and lightly oil
a 9×5-inch loaf pan.

In a large bowl, whisk together the mashed
banana, almond milk, sugar, olive oil, and
vanilla.

In a medium bowl, whisk together the
all-purpose, whole wheat, and almond flours,
the cocoa powder, baking powder, cinnamon,
salt, baking soda, and nutmeg.

Add the dry ingredients to the wet
ingredients and stir until just combined.
Fold in the chocolate chips and pour into
the prepared pan.

Bake for 45 to 60 minutes, or until a toothpick
inserted in the center comes out clean.

SERVES 8

VEGAN

MIX & MATCH
TAHINI COOKIES

BASE COOKIE RECIPE

2 cups all-purpose flour, spooned and leveled (see page 23)

1½ teaspoons baking powder

1 teaspoon sea salt

½ teaspoon baking soda

1 cup packed brown sugar

½ cup melted coconut oil

⅓ cup runny tahini

6 tablespoons water

2 teaspoons vanilla extract

1 heaping cup dark chocolate chips

Preheat the oven to 350°F and line two baking sheets with parchment paper.

In a medium bowl, whisk together the flour, baking powder, salt, and baking soda.

In a large bowl, whisk together the brown sugar, coconut oil, tahini, water, and vanilla until smooth.

Add the dry ingredients to the wet ingredients and use a spatula to combine. Fold in the chocolate chips. Use a 2-tablespoon cookie scoop to scoop the dough onto the baking sheets. Bake, one sheet at a time, for 12 to 14 minutes. Remove from the oven and let cool on the baking sheet for at least 10 minutes.

MAKES ABOUT 18 COOKIES

1

TRAIL MIX COOKIE VARIATION

Alter the base recipe:

Use dark brown sugar.

Reduce the chocolate chips to ½ cup.

Mix into the dough:

½ cup dried cranberries

½ cup chopped cashews

½ cup pepitas

½ cup shredded coconut

Top with:

Flaky sea salt

2

LEMON COOKIE VARIATION

Alter the base recipe:

Omit the chocolate chips.

Replace the water with lemon juice.

Mix into the wet ingredients:

2 tablespoons lemon zest

Glaze with:

½ cup powdered sugar

1 tablespoon fresh lemon juice

Sprinkle with:

Zest of 1 lemon

3

SESAME COOKIE VARIATION

Alter the base recipe:

Omit the chocolate chips.

Mix into the dry ingredients:

½ teaspoon cinnamon

¼ teaspoon ground cardamom

¼ teaspoon ground ginger

Roll cookie dough balls in:

Black and white sesame seeds

4

DOUBLE CHOCOLATE COOKIE VARIATION

Alter the base recipe:

Reduce the flour to 1¾ cups.

Use runny natural peanut butter instead of tahini.

Mix into the dry ingredients:

¼ cup unsweetened cocoa powder

Top with:

Flaky sea salt

TIP: *This dough freezes well! Portion it into scoops and freeze on a parchment paper–lined baking sheet for 2 hours. Transfer the dough balls to a freezer bag or container and freeze for up to 3 months. To bake, place the frozen cookie dough balls on a parchment-lined baking sheet, preheat the oven to 350°F, and bake for 14 minutes.*

Freezer Carrot Cake Bars

In an ideal world, I'd have a pan of these bars in my freezer at all times. To me, they're the perfect way to satisfy an afternoon craving. With their rich cashew "frosting" and nutty carrot base, they're plenty decadent and sweet, but they're made with wholesome ingredients like nuts, dates, and maple syrup. If the bars are too firm to eat straight from the freezer, allow them to sit at room temperature for 10 minutes before digging in.

CARROT LAYER

12 soft Medjool dates, pitted

1½ cups chopped carrots

1 cup shredded coconut

1 cup walnuts

1 teaspoon cinnamon

½ teaspoon nutmeg

Heaping ¼ teaspoon sea salt

CASHEW FROSTING LAYER

1½ cups raw cashews*

½ cup full-fat coconut milk

¼ cup maple syrup

1 tablespoon fresh lemon juice

1 teaspoon vanilla extract

¼ teaspoon sea salt

Line a 9×5-inch loaf pan with parchment paper.

Make the carrot layer: If your dates are not soft, soak them in a small bowl of warm water for 5 to 10 minutes. Pat dry before using.

In a food processor, place the dates, carrots, coconut, walnuts, cinnamon, nutmeg, and salt. Pulse until the mixture sticks together when pinched.

Make the cashew frosting layer: In a high-speed blender, place the cashews, coconut milk, maple syrup, lemon juice, vanilla, and salt and blend until smooth and creamy.

Press the carrot mixture firmly into the prepared pan. Spread the cashew mixture on top. Freeze for 8 hours or overnight. Slice into bars. If they're too firm, let them sit at room temperature for 10 minutes before serving.

If you're not using a high-speed blender, soak the cashews for at least 4 hours, or overnight, before blending them. You may need to blend the frosting longer to achieve a smooth and creamy texture.

SERVES 8

GLUTEN-FREE | VEGAN

No-Bake Avocado Tart

This fun, feel-good dessert gets its gorgeous green color from . . . avocado! Though there aren't any actual key limes here, I like to think of this recipe as a vegan riff on a classic key lime pie. The creamy filling is intensely zesty and bright (you won't taste the avocado, trust me!), and it sets up beautifully after an overnight chill in the fridge.

GRAHAM CRACKER CRUST

9 rectangular graham crackers

5 tablespoons melted coconut oil

¼ cup brown sugar

½ teaspoon sea salt

FILLING

2 avocados

1 (8-ounce) package Kite Hill plain vegan cream cheese

⅔ cup powdered sugar

⅓ cup fresh lime juice

Zest of 2 limes

Lime slices, for garnish (optional)

Nondairy whipped topping, for serving (optional)

Line the bottom of a 9-inch nonstick tart pan with a circle of parchment paper. (A tart pan with a removable bottom is best for this recipe.)

Make the crust: In a food processor, place the graham crackers, coconut oil, brown sugar, and salt and pulse until crumbly and finely ground. Transfer the mixture to the prepared tart pan and use the back of a measuring cup to press it firmly onto the bottom and up the sides. Freeze for 30 minutes.

Make the filling: In a high-speed blender, place the avocados, vegan cream cheese, powdered sugar, and lime juice and zest and blend until creamy.

Spread the filling evenly over the crust and chill the tart overnight in the fridge. If desired, garnish with lime slices and serve with dollops of nondairy whipped topping.

SERVES 8 | **VEGAN:** Use vegan graham crackers.

To get ahead, make the galette
dough up to 2 days in advance.

Apple Rosemary Galettes

Fresh rosemary adds an unexpected savory note to these cinnamon-spiced galettes. I love to lean into this sweet and savory contrast when I serve them, topping them with a scoop of vanilla ice cream and a pinch of flaky sea salt.

2 Granny Smith or Gala apples, cored and thinly sliced

2 tablespoons brown sugar

2 teaspoons cinnamon

1½ teaspoons fresh lemon juice

1 teaspoon cornstarch

Pinch of sea salt

1 large egg white

1 tablespoon water

1 recipe Galette Dough, divided into two equal disks and chilled for at least 1 hour (page 258)

1 tablespoon chopped fresh rosemary

1 tablespoon cold unsalted butter, diced

Coarse sugar, for sprinkling (optional)

Flaky sea salt, for sprinkling (optional)

Vanilla ice cream, for serving

Preheat the oven to 375°F.

Place the apples in a large bowl and toss with the brown sugar, cinnamon, lemon juice, cornstarch, and salt.

In a small bowl, whisk together the egg white and water until thoroughly combined.

Place one of the disks of galette dough between two sheets of parchment paper and roll into an 8- to 9-inch circle. Remove the top sheet and sprinkle half the rosemary around the center of the crust. Arrange half the apples in a pinwheel fashion on the crust with a 1½-inch border all around, leaving any juices behind in the bowl.

Fold the edges of the dough toward the apples, leaving the center of the filling exposed. Dot the exposed apples with half the butter. Using a pastry brush, brush the crust with some of the egg wash. Sprinkle with coarse sugar, if using.

Cut out a circle of parchment paper around the galette and remove the excess paper. Transfer the galette on the parchment circle to one side of a large baking sheet. Repeat with the second disk of dough and the remaining rosemary, apples, butter, egg wash, and coarse sugar, if using.

Bake for 32 to 40 minutes, or until the pastry is golden brown and the apples are soft. Allow to cool for 10 minutes. Sprinkle with flaky sea salt, if using, and serve with vanilla ice cream.

SERVES 6 TO 8

VEGAN: Make the vegan crust variation on page 258. Use vegan butter and brush the crust with almond milk instead of the egg.

Chai Poached Pears

I love to make this light, elegant dessert for fall and winter entertaining. The combination of the tender, chai-spiced pears, creamy cardamom yogurt, and crisp granola is so simple yet so delicious. You can make the components entirely in advance, so when you're ready to serve, all you have to do is plate the pears and eat.

FOR THE PEARS

6 cups water

8 chai tea bags

¼ cup maple syrup

6 star anise

4 cinnamon sticks

1 tablespoon black peppercorns

4 unripe pears, peeled, halved, and seeded

QUICK GRANOLA TOPPING

½ cup whole rolled oats

1½ teaspoons coconut oil

½ teaspoon cinnamon

¼ teaspoon sea salt

½ cup chopped walnuts

1½ tablespoons maple syrup

FOR THE YOGURT

½ cup whole milk Greek yogurt

1½ teaspoons maple syrup

1 teaspoon fresh lemon juice

¼ teaspoon ground cardamom

Poach the pears: Bring the water to a boil in a medium saucepan. Turn off the heat and place the tea bags, maple syrup, star anise, cinnamon, and peppercorns into the pot. Let the tea steep for 5 minutes. Remove the tea bags and bring the water back to a boil. Add the pears, reduce the heat to low, and simmer for 20 to 28 minutes, or until tender. Stir occasionally to make sure the pears are equally submerged. Allow to cool slightly, then transfer the pears and their poaching liquid to an airtight container. Refrigerate for up to 2 days, or until ready to serve.

Make the quick granola topping: Place the oats in a medium skillet over low heat and let them toast for 2 minutes. Add the coconut oil, cinnamon, and salt and cook, stirring occasionally, for 3 minutes. Add the walnuts and maple syrup. Stir to coat and cook for 4 minutes, stirring often. Remove from the heat and set aside. Store at room temperature until ready to serve.

Make the yogurt: In a small bowl, stir together the yogurt, maple syrup, lemon juice, and cardamom. Store in an airtight container in the fridge until ready to serve.

Assemble the dessert on plates with a swoosh of the yogurt, 2 pear halves, and a sprinkle of the granola topping.

SERVES 4

GLUTEN-FREE: Use certified gluten-free oats.

VEGAN: Skip the yogurt and serve the pears with vegan ice cream.

FREEZER FUDGE
FOUR WAYS

— BASE RECIPE —

1 cup smooth nut or seed butter*

¼ cup maple syrup

¼ cup melted coconut oil

1 teaspoon vanilla extract

¼ teaspoon sea salt

Line a 9×5-inch loaf pan with parchment paper.

In a medium bowl, stir together the nut butter, maple syrup, coconut oil, vanilla, and salt. Follow your desired variation on the following page.

Pour into the loaf pan, top with specified toppings, and freeze for at least 2 hours, or until set. Slice and store in the freezer or fridge.

GLUTEN-FREE | VEGAN

— SERVES 12 —

	NUT OR SEED BUTTER	MIX-IN	TOPPING
1 CHOCOLATE ALMOND RASPBERRY	almond butter	⅓ cup unsweetened cocoa powder	chocolate drizzle (see note) ¼ cup freeze-dried raspberries, crushed
2 PEANUT BUTTER CHOCOLATE CHIP	peanut butter	N/A	2 tablespoons mini chocolate chips
3 TAHINI PISTACHIO COCONUT	tahini	½ teaspoon ground ginger	2 tablespoons toasted pistachios, chopped (page 78) 2 teaspoons shredded coconut
4 CASHEW MAPLE SEA SALT	cashew butter	½ teaspoon cinnamon	¼ cup toasted cashews, chopped (page 78) flaky sea salt

Use creamy nut butter with a smooth consistency to make this recipe, not the dry, stiff stuff that you might find at the bottom of a jar.

Note: To make the chocolate drizzle, combine ¼ cup chocolate chips and 1 teaspoon coconut oil in a microwave-safe dish. Microwave 30 to 50 seconds, stirring every 10 seconds, until melted.

Extras

BASIC CASHEW CREAM

1 cup raw cashews

½ cup water

2 tablespoons extra-virgin olive oil

2 tablespoons fresh lemon juice

1 garlic clove, peeled

½ teaspoon sea salt

In a high-speed blender, place the cashews, water, olive oil, lemon juice, garlic, and salt. Blend until smooth.

YIELD: 1 CUP

HOMEMADE HUMMUS

1½ cups cooked chickpeas, drained and rinsed (page 72)

⅓ cup smooth tahini

3 tablespoons fresh lemon juice

2 tablespoons extra-virgin olive oil

1 garlic clove

1 teaspoon ground cumin

½ teaspoon ground cardamom

½ teaspoon sea salt

¼ cup plus 3 tablespoons water, plus more as needed to blend

In a high-speed blender, place the chickpeas, tahini, lemon juice, olive oil, garlic, cumin, cardamom, and salt. Use the blender baton to blend until very smooth, adding more water as needed to blend.

YIELD: ABOUT 1 CUP

MINT CHUTNEY

1½ cups fresh cilantro

1½ cups fresh mint leaves

¼ cup full-fat coconut milk

2 tablespoons avocado oil

2 tablespoons fresh lime juice

1 teaspoon grated fresh ginger

½ serrano pepper, stemmed and chopped

Heaping ¼ teaspoon sea salt

¼ teaspoon cane sugar

¼ teaspoon ground cardamom

¼ teaspoon ground cumin

In a food processor, place the cilantro, mint, coconut milk, avocado oil, lime juice, ginger, serrano, salt, sugar, cardamom, and cumin and pulse until combined.

YIELD: ½ CUP

TAHINI SAUCE

½ cup tahini

¼ cup fresh lemon juice

6 tablespoons water, plus more as needed

1 small garlic clove, grated

½ teaspoon sea salt

In a small bowl, stir together the tahini, lemon juice, water, garlic, and salt. If the sauce is too thick, thin with more water to reach a drizzleable consistency.

YIELD: ABOUT 1 CUP

TAHINI YOGURT

1 cup whole milk Greek yogurt

¼ cup tahini

2 tablespoons fresh lemon juice

2 garlic cloves, grated

1 teaspoon ground cumin

1 teaspoon sea salt

½ teaspoon ground cardamom

1 to 4 tablespoons water, if necessary

In a medium bowl, stir together the yogurt, tahini, lemon juice, garlic, cumin, salt, and cardamom. If the yogurt is too thick, thin with water, 1 tablespoon at a time, to reach your desired consistency.

If making the Savory Tahini Yogurt Bowls (page 27) or the Smoky Eggplant Shakshuka (page 35), the yogurt should be thick and creamy.

If making the Spiced Chickpea Waffles (page 33), Beautiful Root Veggie Salad (page 51), or the Eggplant Sheet Pan Shawarma (page 137), the yogurt should be spreadable but not too thin.

If making a grain bowl (page 66), the yogurt should be drizzleable.

YIELD: 1¼ CUPS

WILD RICE/BROWN RICE BLEND

1 cup dry wild rice/brown rice blend, rinsed well (we like Lundberg)

2 cups water

1 teaspoon extra-virgin olive oil

Combine the rice, water, and olive oil in a medium pot and bring to a boil. Cover, reduce the heat, and simmer for 45 minutes. Remove from the heat and let sit, covered, for 10 minutes. Fluff with a fork.

YIELD: 3 CUPS COOKED

HOMEMADE BREAD CRUMBS

4 ounces stale sourdough bread, crusts removed, torn into small pieces

For fresh bread crumbs, place the bread pieces in a food processor and pulse until crumbly. Use in the Cozy Autumn Pasta Bake (page 125) or in any recipe that calls for fresh bread crumbs.

For toasted bread crumbs, preheat the oven to 375°F and line a baking sheet with parchment paper. Spread the fresh bread crumbs evenly on the baking sheet. Bake for 8 to 15 minutes, or until crisp, tossing halfway through. Use in the Farro & Greens Gratin (page 198) or in any recipe that calls for toasted bread crumbs.

YIELD: 2 CUPS FRESH BREAD CRUMBS OR 1⅓ CUPS TOASTED

HOMEMADE PIZZA DOUGH

¾ cup warm water, plus more as needed

1½ teaspoons maple syrup

1 (¼-ounce) package active dry yeast

2 cups all-purpose flour, spooned and leveled, plus more for kneading (see page 23)

1 teaspoon sea salt

1 tablespoon plus 1 teaspoon extra-virgin olive oil

In a small bowl, stir together the water, maple syrup, and yeast. Set aside for 5 minutes, or until the yeast is foamy.

In the bowl of a stand mixer fitted with the dough hook, place the flour and salt. Mix on medium speed until combined. Add the yeast mixture and 1 tablespoon of the olive oil. Mix on medium speed until the dough forms a ball around the hook, 5 to 6 minutes. If the dough is too dry to form a ball, add water, 1½ teaspoons at a time, until the mixture comes together. If the dough is too sticky, add a little more flour.

Turn the dough out onto a lightly floured surface and gently knead into a smooth ball.

Brush a large bowl with the remaining 1 teaspoon olive oil and place the dough inside. Cover with plastic wrap and set aside to rise until the dough has doubled in size, about 1 hour.

Turn the dough out onto a lightly floured surface. Stretch to fit a 14-inch pizza pan. Top and bake according to the pizza recipe you are using, typically 11 to 15 minutes in a 500°F oven, or until the crust is browned.

YIELD: ABOUT 1 POUND

GALETTE DOUGH

1 cup all-purpose flour, spooned and leveled (see page 23)

1 cup almond flour, spooned and leveled (see page 23)

2 tablespoons cane sugar*

½ teaspoon sea salt

6 tablespoons cold unsalted butter, cubed

¼ cup ice water

In a food processor, place the flour, almond flour, sugar, and salt and pulse to combine. Add the butter and pulse until crumbly. Add the ice water and pulse until the dough comes together. It should still be crumbly but hold together when pinched, and tiny specks of butter should be visible throughout it. Turn out onto a piece of parchment paper and form into one large ball or two equal smaller balls. Flatten each into a 1½-inch-thick disk, wrap in plastic wrap, and chill for at least 1 hour and up to 2 days. Use in the Butternut & Thyme Galette* on page 145 or the Apple Rosemary Galettes on page 251.

For savory galette recipes, such as the Butternut & Thyme Galette on page 145, omit the sugar from the dough.

VEGAN: Use vegan butter and omit the salt.

YIELD: CRUST FOR 1 LARGE OR 2 SMALL GALETTES

VEGAN PARMESAN CHEESE

½ cup raw cashews

2 tablespoons nutritional yeast

½ teaspoon lemon zest

½ teaspoon sea salt

In a small food processor, place the cashews, nutritional yeast, lemon zest, and salt. Pulse until the mixture is coarsely ground and has a soft, crumbly texture.

Store in an airtight container in the fridge for up to 5 days, or freeze for up to 3 months.

Tip: Make this recipe nut-free by replacing the cashews with ¼ cup hemp seeds and ¼ cup raw sunflower seeds.

YIELD: ABOUT ½ CUP

LIST OF VEGAN RECIPES

These recipes are either entirely vegan or can easily be veganized.
For recipes marked with an asterisk (*), look for the vegan substitution
noted at the bottom of each recipe.

THANK YOU

To the Love & Lemons Readers. Without you, there wouldn't be a book! Thank you for cooking along with me over the years through my books, website, and social media. It's so fun to see your creations and to share in your joy of cooking. Your ideas and insights inspire me every day.

To Phoebe Moore, for collaborating with me on this book and every other facet of Love & Lemons. It's a dream to develop and plan recipes with someone who appreciates bright, tangy food as much as I do! Thank you for diligently poring over every detail of every recipe and for spending the last few years helping shape this book into what it turned out to be. You bring such positive energy to every recipe and every project, and I'm honored to work with someone as talented as you every day.

To Trina Bentley, for designing another stunningly beautiful book. It's always a delight to work with you, my friend, and to see what beautiful type treatment will come next.

To my husband, Jack, our son, Ollie, and my extended family, for taste testing so many recipes!

To Lucia Watson, Andrea Magyar, Ashley Tucker, Farin Schlussel, Suzy Swartz, Casey Maloney, and the teams at Avery and Penguin Canada, for being so wonderful to work with yet again, and for your continued support of my vision.

To Judy Linden, your guidance and encouragement through the development of this and all of my books has been invaluable. Having physical books in print has always been a dream of mine, so thank you for making that dream a reality.

To Eva Kolenko, Marian Cooper Cairns, Natalie Drobny, Claire Mack, Suzie Holmstrom, and Brad Knilans, thank you for bringing each recipe to life with such beautiful photography. I'm so humbled to work with such a hardworking and passionate team. You're the best of the best!

To Joanna Keohane, for testing another book with me. I'm so grateful for your detailed and consistent feedback from book to book.

ABOUT THE AUTHORS

Jeanine Donofrio is the creator of *Love and Lemons*, the blog and inspiration behind her first two cookbooks, *Love and Lemons Every Day* and *The Love and Lemons Cookbook*, which *Bon Appétit* hailed as "the most beautiful cookbook we've ever seen." Her passion is creating healthy yet approachable recipes that all types of eaters enjoy. The recipes celebrate how nourishing, fun, and delicious cooking with seasonal, plant-forward ingredients can be. Jeanine has been featured in *The New York Times*, *People*, *Oprah*, and others, and has developed recipes for Whole Foods, KitchenAid, and Le Creuset, among others. She lives in Chicago with her husband, Jack, and their son, Oliver.

Phoebe Moore, collaborator, is the senior editor and recipe developer at *Love and Lemons*. Originally from Wisconsin, she loves the seasonal produce of the Midwest, and she specializes in writing accessible, vegetable-driven recipes. A graduate of Northwestern University, Phoebe lives with her partner in Chicago.